Presented To:

_____

From:

_____

Date:

_____

Walking in the Supernatural

Walking in the Supernatural

Another Cup of Spiritual Java

Chad Dedmon • Kevin Dedmon • Judy Franklin
Beni Johnson • Bill Johnson • Eric Johnson
Banning Liebscher • Paul Manwaring
Chris Overstreet • Danny Silk

DESTINY IMAGE® PUBLISHERS, INC.

PO Box 310, Shippensburg, PA 17257-0310

"Promoting Inspired Lives."

This book and all other Destiny Image, Revival Press, MercyPlace, Fresh Bread, Destiny Image Fiction, and Treasure House books are available at Christian bookstores and distributors worldwide.

For a U.S. bookstore nearest you, call 1-800-722-6774.

For more information on foreign distributors, call 717-532-3040.

Reach us on the Internet: www.destinyimage.com.

ISBN 13 TP: 978-0-7684-4077-5

ISBN 13 Ebook: 978-0-7684-8909-5

For Worldwide Distribution, Printed in the U.S.A.

1 2 3 4 5 6 7 8 / 16 15 14 13 12

CONTENTS

Introduction—*Bill Johnson* 9

Chapter 1   Spiritual Inheritance—*Bill Johnson* 13

Chapter 2   Coffee—*Eric Johnson* 19

Chapter 3   Supernatural Culture—*Danny Silk* 25

Chapter 4   How to Unlock Heaven—*Kevin Dedmon* 31

Chapter 5   Lovers Make a Difference—*Chris Overstreet* 37

Chapter 6   Are You a Chevette or a
            Lamborghini?—*Banning Liebscher* 43

Chapter 7   Too Stupid to be Loved—*Judy Franklin* 49

Chapter 8   Working Out in the Spirit—*Chad Dedmon* 55

Chapter 9   Heal the Brokenhearted—*Beni Johnson* 61

Chapter 10 Angels—*Bill Johnson* 67

Chapter 11 Resonating With Jesus' Joy—*Paul Manwaring* 73

Chapter 12 He Gets to Do Something—*Kevin Dedmon* 79

Chapter 13 Faith Is Spelled R-I-S-K—*Chris Overstreet* 83

Chapter 14 What Is Normal?—*Danny Silk* 89

Chapter 15 No Fear Zone—*Beni Johnson* 95

Chapter 16 Taking Captive Every Scary Thought—*Chad Dedmon* . . .101

Chapter 17   A Setup for Success—*Bill Johnson* 107

Chapter 18   Fear vs. Love—*Danny Silk*. 113

Chapter 19   Revelation Beyond Information—*Banning Liebscher* 119

Chapter 20   Knowing God—*Judy Franklin*. 125

Chapter 21   Power of the Presence—*Chris Overstreet*. 131

Chapter 22   A Fruit-Driven Life—*Eric Johnson* 137

Chapter 23   Glory!—*Paul Manwaring*. 143

Chapter 24   Supernaturally Natural—*Judy Franklin* 149

Chapter 25   Encounter—*Beni Johnson* .155

Chapter 26   Read to Have a God Encounter—*Bill Johnson* 161

Chapter 27   Lifeguards Must Be Swimmers—*Banning Liebscher* 167

Chapter 28   We Are Physician's Assistants—*Kevin Dedmon* 173

Chapter 29   Does the Kingdom Need Revival?—*Eric Johnson* 179

Chapter 30   Shekinah Glory—*Paul Manwaring* 185

Chapter 31   Post-Katrina Miracles—*Chad Dedmon* 191

Chapter 32   Signs That Make You Wonder—*Bill Johnson* 197

Chapter 33   Revival Messiness—*Danny Silk*. 203

Chapter 34   Fountain or Cistern?—*Judy Franklin*. 209

Chapter 35   Start Your Own Heritage—*Eric Johnson* 215

Chapter 36   Prayer That Works—*Kevin Dedmon* 221

Chapter 37   Mantle—or More?—*Bill Johnson*. 227

Chapter 38   All in a Day's Work—*Banning Liebscher* 233

Chapter 39   Waiting for the Bridegroom—*Paul Manwaring* 239

Chapter 40   Watch Over Your Heart—*Bill Johnson* 245

INTRODUCTION

Bill Johnson

O NE OF MY PRIMARY jobs is to teach Christians how to discover and spend their inheritance. This basically means teaching people to use the unlimited promises given to us by God to bring about a manifestation of His dominion for the sake of humanity. This is always recognized through purity and power and is motivated by God's love.

I start with my church family at Bethel Church in Redding, California, where my wife, Beni, and I serve as senior pastors. Then, with the energetic help of many anointed co-leaders, we bring God's message to the wider field of the worldwide Church. We offer people tastes of the Kingdom, over and over, with endless variations. We are like Holy Spirit baristas offering (free) samples of our Father's excellent coffee, educating people to appreciate the good stuff and how to bring others into the same experience. As we develop a thriving culture of freely distributing the generous grace of God, we ourselves imbibe, enjoying the unique blend of revitalization and relaxation that can come only from well-paced cups of true "spiritual java."

Too much of the Church has left the riches of Heaven sitting in the bank, thinking that we only get them when we die and go there. The belief that Heaven is entirely a future reality has reduced far too many of God's declarations in Scripture to positional truths that people acknowledge but never experience. It is time for that to change.

Many believers stay immature because they never progress beyond the revelation that they are sinners saved by grace. By "progress" I don't mean "to leave behind," but rather "to build upon." Those who progress are those who understand that God's highest purpose was not merely to forgive us of sin. It was so that He could invite us back into an intimate family relationship with Him—sons and daughters, full heirs. John 1:12 says we have the right to *become* the children of God. When God invites us into relationship with Him, He is inviting us into a process of becoming, of transformation.

This transformation can be measured in our lives because in Jesus Christ we have the model: *"For whom He foreknew, He also predestined to be conformed to the image of His Son, that He might be the firstborn among many brethren"* (Rom. 8:29). We become like Christ, our Elder Brother. We are destined to be fully restored to the image and likeness of God, in which we were originally created. Through salvation, we have also been restored to our original purpose: *"For we are His workmanship, created in Christ Jesus for good works, which God prepared beforehand that we should walk in them"* (Eph. 2:10).

Works cannot save us, but unless we manifest the fruit of good works in our lives, we lack the evidence that identifies us as new creations in Christ. What kinds of good works? It is far too easy to reduce Jesus' teaching to what is humanly possible. Besides urging us to feed the poor, clothe the naked, and visit those in need, Jesus specifically used the term *good works* to describe the miracles, signs, and wonders He performed. He didn't design a new hearing aid or train a guide dog. He healed the deaf and the blind. His good works not only revealed Jesus to be the Christ, they also revealed the nature of His relationship with His Father (see John 14:8-12). Jesus' words bring us on board with Him: *"Most assuredly, I say to you, he who believes in Me, the works that I do he will do also; and greater works than these he will do, because I go to My Father"* (John 14:12).

It can't be stated more plainly. Those who believe in Him will demonstrate signs and wonders. Even better, those who believe will walk in the same kind of relationship with the Father and possess the same anointing of the Spirit as He did. We are called to minister as Jesus ministered because, through His death and resurrection, we have access to everything He had available to Him to do good works. He says to us: "...*As the Father has sent Me, I also send you*" (John 20:21).

He still intends to establish His Kingdom on the earth by co-laboring with His children. He could easily take dominion of the earth in a moment, but His glory and love are most fully expressed when His rule is extended through His covenant relationship with those He made in His image.

Some people have proposed a version of covenantal history based on the failure of humanity rather than the nature of God. Seminarians and historians are taught that Christian revivals typically last two to six years. Revivals, this view suggests, occur mainly to give the Church a shot in the arm, after which everyone should expect business as usual to resume. Historically, this is accurate. But the conclusion is not. The will of God then becomes defined through what the Church has done instead of what God has made available.

God is abundantly good all the time, and His covenant of love endures forever. Because of these qualities He has purposed to fill His earth with people made in His image, walking in right relationship with Him, and exercising their delegated authority over the earth. That is what His Kingdom looks like. This is the normal Christian life. Anything less is going backward.

In revival, the outpouring of the Holy Spirit brings an invasion of the presence of the King of Heaven, which displaces the prince of darkness. People experience the life and power of the Kingdom. Bodies are healed, souls are delivered and saved, believers grow in unity, and ultimately society and the earth are transformed.

True revival not only calls people to pursue God, but also to pursue their purpose in history and to partner with Him in establishing His dominion over all things. The Holy Spirit doesn't come to give us a shot in the arm; He comes to help us run the race to the end and pass the baton to the next generation with the intent that Kingdom momentum will increase with each succeeding generation.

Chapter 1

SPIRITUAL INHERITANCE

Bill Johnson

WHAT IS THE PURPOSE of a natural inheritance? To give children a leg up so they don't have to start where their parents started. Those who are blessed enough to leave something significant to their children give them a head start, with the hope that they will go farther faster during their lifetimes. In this way, one generation provides a boost for the next. A spiritual inheritance works the same way. It enables the next generation to start where the previous generation left off.

The Lord wants us to wake up to this principle, which is one of the most significant and yet overlooked principles in the Christian life. He wants generations to pass on their spiritual inheritances.

You see, with an inheritance we get for free what someone else paid for. We can inherit graces from the Lord without going through some of the processes a previous generation had to go through.

A spiritual inheritance is meant to make us more effective and efficient in our representation of the King and His Kingdom. It's not for our gratification. Yes, it's delightful, enjoyable, pleasant, and encouraging. But it's not simply for our personal consumption. A spiritual inheritance is meant to open doors so that the King and His Kingdom have influence in more places than before.

While a natural inheritance gives us something we did not have before, a spiritual inheritance pulls back the curtain and reveals what we already have permission to possess. That's why Moses said, "*...but those things which are revealed belong to us and to our children forever...*" (Deut. 29:29). Receiving a spiritual inheritance is like learning that years ago somebody put ten million dollars in your bank account. You had the money all along, but now you are at liberty to spend it, because you have learned about the money that belongs to you.

This is what Paul was trying to get across when he wrote:

> *Therefore let no one boast in men. For all things are yours: whether Paul or Apollos or Cephas, or the world or life or death, or things present or things to come—all are yours. And you are Christ's, and Christ is God's* (1 Corinthians 3:21-23).

The tragedy of history is that revival has come and gone, and subsequent generations have built monuments to the achievements of the previous generation without completely receiving and occupying their inherited spiritual territory. They inherited the territory for free, but they have not paid the price to develop it, so they have lost it.

The quickest way to lose something is to take a defensive posture in which we only maintain what we have instead of working to increase it. We learn this in the parable of the talents, when God condemned the man who did not put his money to use, but buried it in the ground. (See Matthew 25.) To choose not to expand and increase is to choose to lose the very thing we are trying to protect.

We were never intended to start over from scratch every two or three generations. God wants to put each generation at a higher level than the previous one. Every generation has a ceiling experience that becomes the next generation's floor. The things we take for granted today cost the previous generation tremendously.

How are we to move into new territory? By building on precept after precept. Truth is progressive and multi-dimensional. It evolves constantly as we grow, though it never evolves into something that contradicts its foundations. Measures and levels of anointing cause the reality of the Scripture to change for us.

A new generation is now forming. I pray and believe that this generation will walk in an anointing that has never been known before, including by the disciples. With a superior revelation, this generation will not be bounded by the natural principles such as harvest seasons or "seasons of revival." Jesus said, *"...Behold, I say to you, lift up your eyes and look at the fields, for they are already white for harvest"* (John 4:35). In the Kingdom, every day should be harvest day, and people who seem impossible to win to the Lord should be won instantly, without any sowing or preparation or tending.

With a low-grade anointing and revelation, we have to live by natural principles and restrictions to get spiritual results. But Jesus said, *"Lift up your eyes,"* meaning, "With the way you are seeing things right now, you cannot operate on the revelation I want to give you." We have to set our sights much higher and take advantage of the anointing and revelation of those who have gone before us.

Jesus carried the Spirit without measure. The more you and I become empowered and directed by the Spirit of God, the more our lives should release spiritual realities.

POINTS TO PONDER

1. Have you ever before considered the present-tense reality of your personal inheritance from Heaven? How have you experienced it? With whom have you sought to grow in your inheritance?

    ....

    ....

    ....

    ....

2. Have you ever considered passing on this spiritual inheritance to the next generation? What do you think that would look like? What is your biggest current challenge in this regard?

    ....

    ....

    ....

    ....

3. Have you been guilty of occupying hard-won territory, but not expanding it or developing it? How can you describe your "track record"? Can you improve it?

    ....

    ....

    ....

    ....

MEDITATION

It is the Lord's desire that the supernatural territory you occupy and the realms of life in which you consistently demonstrate His authority would grow larger and more powerful as you walk with His Spirit—and as you pass it on to the next generation.

Humble yourself before God, asking Him to show you the reality of your situation, as well as what to do about it. Be open to whatever He may want to tell you. He may commend you. He may correct you. Either way, He loves you and wants to see you walking in your full destiny.

Chapter 2

COFFEE

Eric Johnson

A NUMBER OF YEARS AGO, I was reading my Bible one night before going to bed, and I felt the Lord tell me, "I'm going to take you to the mountaintop to teach you something." Then, for the next 18 months, I had a unique and fun experience, and it had to do with coffee (which is one of the finer things in life).

It started one night in the drive-thru at Starbucks. I had placed my order for a cup of pure black goodness—coffee. When I pulled up to the window, the guy handed me my drink and said, "The car in front of you paid for your drink." I thought, *That's nice.*

The very next week, I was in the same drive-thru waiting for my cup of pure goodness, but this time the line was taking an abnormally long time. Finally, I got to the window to receive my drink, but this time the guy in the window said, "Sir, we are so sorry. We had an accident in here tonight, so this drink is on the house tonight." So now two visits in a row, I didn't have to pay for my cup of coffee.

This went on for 18 months. That whole time, it was extremely hard for me to purchase a cup of coffee or to buy a bag of coffee.

Another time, I was having a 15-minute meeting with a staff member at the church. Since it was quick meeting, we met in the stairway at the end of a long hallway. At the opposite end of the hallway is our *HeBrews* coffee shop. As we were meeting, I was thinking to myself, *I would really like a cup of coffee.* I started planning that after this little meeting, I would walk down to *HeBrews* to get a cup. As these thoughts filled my head, a gentleman walked up to us with a cup of coffee in hand and said, "I have no idea why I bought this cup of coffee; I don't even drink coffee. Would one of you want this?" I quickly looked over to the guy I was meeting with, and he didn't want it, so I gladly received the cup of coffee.

As these 18 months began to unfold, they exposed something in me—the part of my identity that tended to neglect something when I have had enough of it. This experience taught me to receive beyond my comfort levels, and that I do not have permission to stop something when I've had enough. I needed to learn to live in abundance.

When we begin to move into a new understanding of abundance, it's typical to start having thoughts like, *I don't deserve this,* or *Why me?* We're right, but this abundance is not hinging on that. It's hinging on the fact that He is so extravagant and that we don't have a right to turn down or turn off the abundance once it's on.

What we must not forget is that it's His goodness that leads us to repentance (see Rom. 2:4). We tend to reverse that verse and live our lives thinking that repentance leads us to His goodness. God designed it so that He would unleash His goodness on us, and it would then reveal our need to repent and change the way we think. It was never about what we could do.

If we expect to be entrusted with His goodness, then we must learn not to reject it.

Sometimes I have been so surrounded by abundance and favor that it has made me really insecure. It has humbled me beyond previous experience. What I am learning is that I am responsible to keep myself positioned under it. This is what Paul was talking about when he wrote: *"Even if we, or an angel from heaven, preach any other gospel to you than what we have preached to you, let him be accursed"* (Gal. 1:8). He was saying, "Don't let any other teaching remove you from this favor and grace that I told you about because it's human nature to 'repent' in order to get more of His goodness. If that were the case, then grace would be based on your ability—and you would get proud."

If we choose to live under the lie that His goodness is based on what we can do, then we have reduced ourselves to what is humanly possible. If we embrace grace, we will defy all logic and reason, the realm of physics and the parameters of reality, and do what is humanly impossible.

In his epistles, Paul used some phrases that give us a peek into the revelation that he walked in regarding this Gospel of grace. The phrases are *beggarly elements* and *basic principles* (see Gal. 4:9; Col. 2:8). Paul made a strong argument that we are not subject to the religious and world system.

Something took place when Jesus was walking on water (see Matt. 14:25). Not only was He doing something simply amazing, but He was displaying something that we have access to. Jesus was demonstrating that there is a realm of authority that will enable us to defy the natural laws of the universe. Not only did He defy the logic and reason of the human mind, but He displayed the possibility of living in a realm where the "elements" of this world are inferior to Kingdom authority.

I am strongly convinced that a day is coming when the Body of believers will be so actively released into a realm of authority that it will stun the courts of Heaven. I can't help but think of what Jesus was implying when He said, "You will do far greater things than I ever did" (see John 14:12). That is a pretty astounding statement considering what Jesus did in His lifetime. Now let's embrace our place in grace!

POINTS TO PONDER

1. What did God teach Eric about positioning himself under abundance? Put the lesson in your own words. Why did God want to teach Eric about this?

    ....

    ....

    ....

    ....

2. Has God ever initiated a "learning season" in your life? If so, what did He teach you? Did you have anything to do with initiating the learning process? Is this good?

    ....

    ....

    ....

    ....

MEDITATION

There is no end to the number of life-giving lessons that God wants to teach you. Each one of us was designed to be a river of continual life. Upon becoming a believer, you were ushered into a constant flow of life, and it is your responsibility to stay in that place.

Nowhere in the Bible does it say, "When you've had enough, you can turn it off." In fact, it says to keep asking for more (see Zech. 10:1). Just when you think you have enough, God starts saying, "You can't even begin to scratch the surface of what I have for you."

Abandon your insufficient comprehension of God's goodness. Position yourself gratefully under God's abundance.

Chapter 3

SUPERNATURAL CULTURE

Danny Silk

I F YOU'VE HEARD OF Bethel Church in Redding, California, chances are that you've heard testimonies of the supernatural happenings that take place there on a regular basis, particularly miracles of healing. What you may not have heard is that these supernatural events are directly related to the supernatural culture that the community of saints at Bethel has been developing for over a decade.

The heart of this culture is the conviction that Jesus modeled the Christian life for us. Jesus explained that all the supernatural things that happened through Him flowed directly from His intimate connection with His Father, and that same connection is what He came to give us through His death and resurrection. Sustaining a supernatural lifestyle, one in which signs and wonders follow us, is therefore, totally dependent on living out of our true identities as sons and daughters of God.

Armed with these truths, the leaders at Bethel understand that their primary role is to empower the saints to know God and to walk in the fullness of who He says they are. As these core values have been taught and demonstrated, a group of people has grown up with faith and courage to bring Heaven to earth.

One of the primary values at Bethel is *honor*. Honor creates life-giving and life-promoting relationships. The key to honor is accurately acknowledging who people are, and we can do this only when we recognize their God-given identities and roles.

This is what we see in the statement of Jesus:

> *He who receives a prophet in the name of a prophet shall receive a prophet's reward. And he who receives a righteous man in the name of a righteous man shall receive a righteous man's reward* (Matthew 10:41).

Names and titles are important. Mother, father, son, daughter, apostle, prophet, Christian, human being—such names define a person's role and identity and, when used correctly, establish God-designed relationships in which specific rewards are given and received to build and strengthen us.

A culture of honor is created as a community of people learns to discern and receive people in their God-given identities. The names "apostle," "prophet," "teacher," "pastor," and "evangelist" and their distinctive anointings, mindsets, and gifts create a network of relationships designed to bring the focus and priorities of Heaven to earth. Names like "free sons" and "children of light" define the way we must honor and relate to one another, particularly when addressing areas of behavior and relationships that need discipline and restoration. Descriptive names like "royalty," "wealthy," and "benefactor" shape our relationships with our resources and with the wider community that the Church is called to bless and encounter with the love and power of Heaven.

In a culture of honor, leaders lead with honor by courageously treating people according to the names God gives them and not according to the aliases they receive from other people. They treat them as free sons and daughters, not slaves; as righteous, not sinners; as wealthy, not poor. Leaders also acknowledge their interdependence on the diverse anointings God has distributed among His leaders and their design for functioning as a team that creates a "funnel" from Heaven to earth.

They lead in teaching and preaching a Gospel that accurately acknowledges God's identity as good, as love, as *shalom*, and look for clear manifestations of these realities as signs that God's presence is truly welcome in the culture.

In the safety and freedom that grow as His presence grows, leaders lead by developing ways to help people get along with one another in a free culture. They have tools for confrontation that are congruent with people's God-given identities and are motivated by the passion to protect and grow the connections that God is building.

Finally, leaders in a culture of honor naturally lead their people in extending the honor of the Kingdom to the wider community, creating ways for our cities to experience the life that is flowing in the body of people.

The clear fruit of establishing a culture of honor is that the resurrection life of God begins to flow into people's lives, homes, and communities, bringing healing, restoration, blessing, joy, hope, and wholeness. If we are not seeing this fruit, then we must ask ourselves whether we are truly honoring those around us as we ought.

POINTS TO PONDER

1. A culture of honor sounds like a good place to live, a place where you could really flourish. But learning to honor others will bring you up against situations that will challenge your love. How do you show honor to someone who has sinned against others? How do you show honor to someone who repudiates you?

   ....

   ....

   ....

   ....

2. Have you experienced a culture of mutual honor at any time in your life? If so, what was it like? How were you and others freer to share God's love than you had been before?

   ....

   ....

   ....

   ....

3. Can a person begin to develop a contagious culture of honor without being surrounded by like-minded people? What reasons can you give to support your opinion?

   ....

   ....

   ....

   ....

MEDITATION

A culture of honor is a way of describing what the heart-culture of a church must be in order to host and sustain a long-term visitation from God. Spiritual fruitfulness and wisdom spring up from the well-fertilized and watered soil of mutual honor.

Whether or not you are part of a church that values an intentional culture of honor, ask God to show you what personal steps you can take to contribute to a culture of honor in the worldwide Body of Christ.

Chapter 4

HOW TO UNLOCK HEAVEN

Kevin Dedmon

I ALWAYS THOUGHT THAT PEOPLE in public ministry had a special, supernatural anointing and ability that normal, everyday Christians could not access. However, when I entered public ministry in 1981, that myth soon vanished. I found that I had no greater supernatural ability than I had before, even though I was now a pastor. Neither did the other pastors I knew. In fact, many did not rely on supernatural empowerment at all, but on their own inherent charisma and natural talent.

Many of the great revivalists throughout history began as ordinary Christians with very normal backgrounds much like mine. For example, Smith Wigglesworth was a plumber before becoming one of the generals of the healing revival of the 1900s. John G. Lake was an executive in the insurance industry before becoming one of the greatest healing revivalists of the early 1900s. William Branham worked for an electric company in maintenance and as a repairman and never even graduated from high school, yet he saw some of the most amazing miracles in the history of the Church.

Maria Woodworth-Etter was a stay-at-home mother before she helped usher in the Pentecostal movement as an itinerant preacher who healed the sick wherever she went. Aimee Semple McPherson was the widow of a missionary and only reluctantly accepted an invitation to preach on a ship when no one else could be found.

Jesus did not ask for degrees and pedigrees when He began to train the disciples (see Luke 6:12-16). In fact, He specifically called those who were common by worldly standards, normal people representing every walk of life. (See First Corinthians 1:26-29.)

Soon I realized that I had the same invitation to change the world as the disciples of the Bible and the generals of revival did throughout Church history. After all, what did they have that I do not have? I have the same Spirit they had. I have the same authority. The only difference is that they discovered the keys to unlock Heaven, which allowed them to live a naturally supernatural lifestyle.

Jesus commanded all of His disciples to *"preach, saying, 'The kingdom of heaven is at hand.' Heal the sick, cleanse the lepers, raise the dead, cast out demons..."* (Matt. 10:7-8). The command is still the same for us as it was for the first disciples. Each one of us, no matter how ordinary we may feel, is called to bring the Kingdom to earth in extraordinary ways.

Interestingly, Jesus did not look at John, the disciple of intimacy, and say, "Oh, I forgot, John, you are more of an introvert. I know that you much more prefer the 'secret place' of intimacy, where you can lay your head on my shoulder. I know that you are not an evangelist. Don't worry about going; I'll just send Peter. He's an extrovert. He'll say anything to anyone and take risk at every opportunity!" No, Jesus sent out all 12, regardless of personality, temperament, or gifting. He sent out the introvert with the extrovert, the timid with the bold, and the ungifted with the gifted to preach and demonstrate the Good News.

In the same way, God has called each one of us to live an extraordinarily supernatural life. As I have developed a supernatural lifestyle, I have always felt intimidated and inadequate as I have ventured into new realms of risk. I have always been very conscious of my incompetence.

I have also come to the conclusion that, if God can use me to do the extraordinary, then He can use anyone.

God intends each believer to be a carrier of His extraordinary Kingdom, as the apostle Paul teaches in Colossians 1:27, "[It is]*Christ in you, the hope of glory.*" Therefore, we are called to live a naturally supernatural life because *"Jesus Christ is the same yesterday, today, and forever"* (Heb. 13:8).

POINTS TO PONDER

1. Think about the fact that the Kingdom of God, which seems too extraordinary here on earth, is ordinary in Heaven. Does that help you bridge the gap you often feel between your ordinary life and a life of abundant supernatural overflow? What practical steps can you take to make sure that you keep growing and moving in supernatural Kingdom power?

   ....

   ....

   ....

   ....

2. Who was the first person you became aware of who was a walking manifestation of heavenly grace and supernatural power? What do you have in common with this person?

   ....

   ....

   ....

   ....

3. Do you believe that God wants to use you more than you want to be used by Him? What is your primary motive for wanting more of His Kingdom in your life?

   ....

   ....

   ....

   ....

MEDITATION

Throughout the Bible we find account after account of God using people who felt inadequate to do His will. For example, think of Gideon's feelings of inadequacy when God called him to lead the way in defeating a formidable enemy with just a few seemingly insufficient resources (see Judg. 6). When God told him to rise up and do something about the injustices that were being levied on the people of God, all he could say was, "I am the smallest. I am the weakest. What can I do?"

The key to living a naturally supernatural life is to know that ordinary in the Kingdom is extraordinary on earth. The Kingdom of God is ordinarily extraordinary in itself, and this extraordinary Kingdom is within us (see Luke 17:21). Therefore, it should be normal that, when we release the Kingdom of God through our lives, extraordinary things begin to happen, things such as miracles, healings, prophetic insights into circumstances and people's lives, and deliverances of the oppressed.

Ask God's Spirit to draw His extraordinary Kingdom out of your ordinary self. Ask Him to enable you to sail with the wind of His Spirit wherever He may take you.

Chapter 5

LOVERS MAKE A DIFFERENCE

Chris Overstreet

To KNOW GOD'S LOVE is to experience God's love. What we experience, we are able to give away to others. Mike Bickle, director of the International House of Prayer in Kansas City, says that lovers always get more work done than do workers! God's love changes the world inside of us, which in turn changes the world around us.

Love is active, not passive. *"For God so loved the world that He gave His only begotten Son, that whoever believes in Him should not perish but have everlasting life"* (John 3:16). God's love must be the foundation of everything we do in our lives. We love others with God's heart of love because He first loved us. It's the love of Christ that compels us to action.

In 1996, I found myself at the bottom of a pit. While in a jail cell, I kneeled all 375 pounds of my weight onto my knees as I asked Jesus Christ to come into my heart and forgive me of all my sins. That day, I felt true love, and that love is now what I get to give away to the world.

Many people try to muster up enough courage to share Christ with others, to prophesy, and to heal the sick. When we keep things simple, with our motivation being love, that love will open the door for other miraculous things to take place in and through our lives.

Just as Jesus came to destroy the works of the devil (see 1 John 3:8), so are we sent to destroy the works of the devil. The works of the devil are the works that try to keep us from experiencing everything that Christ came to give us: abundant life on earth as it is in Heaven. Sin, sickness, and disease are from the devil and not from God. God is good, and the devil is bad. God is full of truth. The devil is a liar.

When our eyes are continually focused on Heaven, we live from a heavenly perspective. God is good, and in Heaven there is no sickness, sin, poverty, depression, anxiety, fear, pain, or rejection. What we see in Heaven is health, restoration, peace, redemption, divine relationship with Jesus, heavenly encounters, hope, joy, and prosperity.

Colossians 3:2 says, *"Set your mind on things above, not on things on the earth."* To live from Heaven's reality is to have our minds developed into a Kingdom-culture mindset. The Holy Spirit is our helper, and He is committed to helping us transform the way that we think so that we line up with His heavenly worldview. We must be filled with the Holy Spirit and able to allow Him to work through us freely. The Holy Spirit empowers us to change our minds to a Kingdom mindset on an ongoing basis:

> *Do not be conformed to this world, but be transformed by the renewing of your mind, that you may prove what is that good and acceptable and perfect will of God* (Romans 12:2).

By having a transformed mind, we can know the will of God, which lets us demonstrate His will on earth. This lets us respond to people's needs without questioning God's intent.

When we experience God, it changes the way we see the world and ourselves—what we see in us and around us. The same Spirit that raised Christ from the grave lives inside of us, and that Spirit longs to get out of us. The Holy Spirit enables us to become a walking encounter wherever we go.

When the believers were filled with the Spirit on Pentecost, they could not help but speak the word of God boldly. They had an encounter that changed their mindsets and allowed them to become active encounters themselves. The baptism of the Holy Spirit, which filled the believers, empowered them to be bold witnesses. The true baptism of the Holy Spirit comes not only so that we can pray in tongues. The true baptism empowers us to be witnesses. Peter was empowered to overcome his past insecurities and fears. The one who denied Jesus three times was now the one filled with the Holy Spirit and fire, giving a mass call for the Jews to come to the knowledge of the Lord Jesus Christ (see Acts 2:14-41).

Willingness to be an encounter for others changes the way we live. No longer do we live for ourselves. Instead, we live for others. It opens up our eyes to opportunities around us. As we learn to live in God's presence, we realize who we really are. When we begin to see ourselves the way He sees us, our minds are changed to walk in the identity He has given us.

POINTS TO PONDER

1. Why do lovers accomplish more for the Kingdom?

    ....

    ....

    ....

    ....

2. Think of a time when your experience of God's love was very strong. Did you want to keep it to yourself? What did you do?

    ....

    ....

    ....

    ....

3. Just as Jesus came to destroy the works of the devil, so are you sent to destroy the works of the devil. What works of the devil surround you right now? (In other words, by means of what sin, sickness, or other works is he trying to keep you or others from experiencing the abundant life on earth as it is in Heaven?) What is God telling you to do about each of these impediments?

    ....

    ....

    ....

    ....

MEDITATION

Reorient your heart and mind toward love. Receive God's love and allow it to overflow to the people He puts in your life.

Pray for yourself and for the believers around you

> *...to know the love of Christ which passes knowledge; that you may be filled with all the fullness of God. Now to Him who is able to do exceedingly abundantly above all that we ask or think, according to the power that works in us, to Him be glory in the church by Christ Jesus to all generations, forever and ever. Amen* (Ephesians 3:19-21).

Chapter 6

ARE YOU A CHEVETTE OR A LAMBORGHINI?

Banning Liebscher

WHEN I WAS 19 years old, I needed a car. My soon-to-be father-in-law called me up one day and offered to give me a 1985 Chevette he owned. I was completely ignorant about cars and thought any vehicle was better than none. However, when I went down to his house to pick up the Chevette, I was in for quite a surprise. Imagine a football helmet with wheels and a steering wheel and less protection, and you're close to the Chevette. He showed me a two-door hatchback with an oxidized, sky-blue paint job. Despite my initial reservations, I was still appreciative and gladly took possession.

On the three-hour trip back to Redding, I quickly learned about my new car. About an hour and a half into the drive, I heard a sudden loud bang. For a moment, I thought a huge rock had struck my car. But when I looked over my right shoulder, I discovered that it wasn't a rock. Rather, one of the back wing windows had just blown off. I drove on, stunned, not knowing what to do. I had never heard of a window tearing out of a car before.

That was just the first of many quirks I had yet to discover. The ceiling fabric drooped inside, so I had to use strategically placed push-pins to reattach it. The hatchback never stayed open, so I made a custom broom handle to prop it up. The passenger door flew open randomly while driving, and the stick shift dislodged. (Whoever was driving would have to find the proper spot and replace it in order to shift again.)

Now, way over on the other end of the car spectrum is a Lamborghini. Recently I met a businessman who owns a Lamborghini Countach, one of three in the world like it, and the only one in North America. This Lamborghini is worth a million dollars. A million dollars! The first question I asked him was, "Where do you park a million-dollar car? Do you just put it into your garage next to the lawnmower and rakes?"

"No, no, no," he replied. "I have a special bubble I park it in." Apparently, you can buy these bubbles in which to store your expensive car. You drive into the bubble, and it seals to keep out all the moisture. I had never heard of a car bubble, probably because they cost more than my car.

I run into way too many Christians who have bought into the lie of insignificance and see themselves like my 1985 Chevette. In their perception, their lives don't seem very valuable, and they see so many things that don't work well. Because they believe they are small, frail, and worthless, they live lives of insignificance.

But the truth is that we are not broken-down Chevettes. We are sleek Lamborghinis.

The Scriptures are filled with statements about the purposes that God has designed for the lives of believers, and none of them are short of awesome. Our identity and our purpose are directly connected. We were created to accomplish great things for God, and He puts the highest value on our lives.

God's first command to people was, *"Be fruitful and multiply..."* (Gen. 1:28). That command is still alive today. Jesus told us to *"make disciples of all the nations"* (Matt. 28:19). This is a big task that can only be accomplished through a people who believe their lives are worthwhile and that they have something positive to contribute to the world around them. Much of the Church has been so overwhelmed with what is happening across the earth that they have concealed themselves in the hope of merely enduring the evil around them. But God didn't tell us just to survive; He commanded us to disciple nations.

Isaiah wrote,

> *Arise, shine; For your light has come! And the glory of the Lord is risen upon you. For behold, the darkness shall cover the earth, and deep darkness the people; But the Lord will arise over you, And His glory will be seen upon you* (Isaiah 60:1-2).

It is true that darkness is covering the earth. But God told us to *"Arise, shine,"* He didn't say, "Shrink away and hide your light in a corner." His response to darkness covering the earth is a people who realize who they are in Jesus and who arise in the earth with the glory of the Lord upon them. Not only does His glory rise on His people, but when His people understand this revelation and stand boldly in the earth, they allow God to shine through them.

God wants to display His goodness, His greatness, and His glory through us. We are called to establish the reign of His Kingdom on the earth—to be light in darkness. But the plan of God can't be carried out without our cooperation, and we won't really be able to collaborate until we embrace the identity and purpose that He has spoken over us.

POINTS TO PONDER

1. Have you sometimes wanted to withdraw from the darkness around you, hoping that you will at least be able to hold on by the skin of your teeth until Jesus returns? Have you sometimes forgotten that you are here to establish God's Kingdom of light? How has the lie of insignificance worked against your ability to "Arise, shine"?

   ....

   ....

   ....

   ....

2. How can you "upgrade" your spiritual self-image? Will counseling or positive self-talk be enough? Will it help to acquire some status symbol or to achieve a victory? How can you move toward agreeing with God's opinion of you?

   ....

   ....

   ....

   ....

MEDITATION

To determine the value of an item, you must find out how much someone will pay for it, and you will value your item according to the highest bid. How much are you worth as a person? To find out, look at the Crucifixion. The cross should send every one of us a glorious message about how highly God values us. He cherished you enough to pay the ultimate price—His Son's life.

For much of the Church, Calvary is mainly about God forgiving our sins. People stop short of understanding and walking in the full purpose for Jesus' death, which was to restore us to relationship with Him and to the identity that He intended for us from the beginning.

To progress in your understanding of God's deep purposes for you, seek ongoing encounters with your Father so that you can hear Him declare over you how He values you. It's OK to be like a small child asking one of his parents for a hug. In fact, it's vital.

Chapter 7

TOO STUPID TO BE LOVED

Judy Franklin

I GREW UP KNOWING THAT my dad did not want me. While other children had cute little nicknames, my nickname was "whang-brain." If I spilled my milk at dinner, my dinner was put on the kitchen floor. I was told I had to eat like a dog because I was sloppy, or I was put in the bathtub with my food. My dad liked my brother and preferred him over me. Whenever he had to take us somewhere, he would tell my brother to come with him and tell me to stay in the car. I knew he was ashamed of me, but I did not understand why.

I wrote Dear Abby once when I was about nine years old and asked her why my dad didn't love me even though I tried to do what was right. The letter was never sent, but my mother found it and gave it to my dad. I can remember sitting on the end of my bed right by the door, listening closely, hoping he would say that he did love me after all. Instead, he bellowed that maybe he could love me if I wasn't so stupid. So that was the problem. I was stupid, and stupid people can't be loved.

It became clear when I was in the first grade that I was not as bright as the other children. But it wasn't until I was in the eighth grade that I was tested and found to have learning disabilities. I was then put in the "mentally retarded" class, as it was called at the time. Yes, I was stupid, and this was why my dad was ashamed of me.

Unfortunately, I never really felt loved by my mother either. My mother was a broken person and was unable to protect me from the meanness of my father. One day, when I was three or four years old, my mother was painting the living room and accidentally left a cup of turpentine on the kitchen table. I awoke from a nap and went into the kitchen. Thinking the cup was filled with water, I drank it. I was rushed to the hospital to have my stomach pumped. After I returned home, my kidneys started to shut down. I found out much later that my mother called a doctor and begged him to come to the house. We didn't have very much money, and she told him she would pay him a dime a month for the rest of her life, which was not easy in the early 1950s. He had compassion; he came and my life was saved. About the time I turned fourteen, my mother became a full-fledged alcoholic; physically, mentally, and emotionally, she was no longer there for anyone.

So I grew up feeling unloved, stupid, and worthless. Of course, we all do stupid things, but it was different for me. Whenever I did something stupid, I felt a constant reminder that I was unlovable. Even after I married and had children, I never believed my husband truly loved me. How could he love me? I still did stupid things. Oh, how I loved my children, but I just knew in my heart that as they grew up, they would realize I was stupid, and they wouldn't love me anymore.

Embarrassed and ashamed of my stupidity, I became quiet and withdrawn. I was afraid that if I talked to people they would quickly figure out my stupidity. I lived afraid of being found out. Silent and hurt, I learned to hide. No one around me knew what I was thinking or feeling. This is how the enemy works. He uses shame and fear to keep us quiet and alone.

Then one day I had a life-changing supernatural encounter with God. I felt, saw, and breathed God's love into me, and it literally changed my life. I was amazed that someone loved me. I absolutely fell in love with Him. At that moment I gained a father, brother, teacher, companion, and friend. No longer was He someone I read about, but someone I knew. He loved me with an incomprehensible love that I could actually experience. Now I knew that

> *...neither death nor life, nor angels nor principalities nor powers, nor things present nor things to come, nor height nor depth, nor any other created thing, shall be able to separate* [me] *from the love of God which is in Christ Jesus* [my] *Lord* (Romans 8:38-39).

I can't say that overcoming rejection was instant for me at this point. However, this was the beginning of my healing process. I'm also not saying that it can't be instantaneous—it can—but for me it has been a process. David wrote, *"When my father and my mother forsake me, then the Lord will take care of me"* (Ps. 27:10).

As I began to understand that my parents had been raised in dysfunctional homes and were rejected themselves, it became much easier for me to forgive them. And forgiveness is the key. I, who have been forgiven so much, was able to forgive my parents for their seeming rejection of me. Now I know I have a Father in Heaven who absolutely loves me and will never reject me.

POINTS TO PONDER

1. Read Psalm 27 in its entirety. What phrase or concept speaks most powerfully to you personally?

   ....

   ....

   ....

   ....

2. Can you explain (even partially) how the love of God has transformed your own emotional and spiritual health (not to mention your mental and physical health)? Can you see a "before and after" difference? How are you a work in progress?

   ....

   ....

   ....

   ....

3. What does this passage of Scripture say to you: *"The love of God has been poured out in our hearts by the Holy Spirit who was given to us"* (Rom. 5:5)?

   ....

   ....

   ....

   ....

MEDITATION

As John put it more than once: *"God is love"* (1 John 4:8,16). His love compels Him to take the initiative with us, to reach out to those He has created, to offer every person a taste of His love. He also encourages those who have already tasted His love to help others find it. Whether the first "taste" comes as a profound peace or a major miraculous event, it is unmistakable and life-altering.

The most important love-initiative that God ever took was to send us His Son, so that we could have full access to Heaven in spite of our many failings.

> *In this the love of God was manifested toward us, that God has sent His only begotten Son into the world, that we might live through Him* (1 John 4:9).

Right now, find a new way to express your appreciation to Him.

Chapter 8

WORKING OUT IN THE SPIRIT

Chad Dedmon

I LOVE HEARING STORIES ABOUT breakthrough and healing. I value these testimonies because they can create momentum and build faith in others for God to do that same thing again. However, it is easy to create a culture of performance when the attention and praise is only given to those people who are producing results.

What about those who take risks that just don't pan out? American culture teaches us that when we take a risk and don't get the desired results, that means we have failed. But I believe God sees risk-taking from a completely different perspective.

Papa God applauds us when we try new things and step out, just as a loving natural father glows with pride when his little baby takes her very first step—and then falls down. We as the Church must begin to acknowledge and encourage those who take their first steps, but have not yet seen any breakthrough. It is imperative that we create a culture within the Church that doesn't merely tolerate risk-takers, but also encourages the whole Body of Christ to take risks in order to advance the Kingdom of God.

Certainly there will always be an uncomfortable tension for those who take risks without seeing results right away. But as we keep stepping forward into faith and partner with the Holy Spirit, we *will* see breakthrough.

Here's an example of what I mean. Not long after an event filled with testimonies about God's power, we did a beach baptism at Dana Point, California. A bunch of junior high students got baptized, and then they decided to pray together to walk on the water. They walked over to the water's edge, grabbed hands, and walked out into the water together.

As they took a few steps, they were all about chest-deep, standing on the ocean floor. However, one of the kids was still on top of the water! He took about five steps above the water and on the sixth step, fell into the water. This young revivalist had been contending to walk on water that past week. He knew what was available to him and kept trying until he saw breakthrough. He knew that after trying something for the first time doesn't work out, you should try again.

John Wimber, a founding leader of the Vineyard churches, prayed for hundreds of people before he saw someone healed. John Wimber and this junior high kid did not base their success upon their circumstances; instead, they were willing to take risks even in the face of no tangible manifestations.

All of us have things in our daily lives that we are contending to see breakthrough for. When we take a risk and don't see immediate results, we cannot lose hope and let thoughts of failure or inadequacy attack us, because God sees risk-taking as success. Our faith-filled persistence will make our circumstances line up with God's Word.

Another aspect of this principle applies to stewarding the gifts of the Spirit. Many people ask me specifically to pray and impart my healing gift to them. In response to their request, I sometimes tell them, "I can pray for you, but this impartation won't become activated in your life until you step out and begin praying for others." An impartation can lie dormant if we don't activate it.

Stewarding the gifts of the Spirit is like working out in the gym. When I was a freshman in high school, I discovered what that was like. Up to then, I had never lifted weights.

On my very first day of working out, I was so determined to gain muscle mass that I worked out every muscle in my body for three and a half hours. When I lifted the bench press for the first time, I couldn't lift very much, and I felt like a wimp in front of all my high school classmates.

That night before going to bed, I put three scoops of protein powder in my glass of milk and thought to myself, *It will only be a matter of days before I look like this guy on the protein powder container.* I woke up in the middle of the night with excruciating calf muscle pain. I tried to stand up, but my body wouldn't let me. As I lay in bed, I tried not to move because when I did, the pain got worse.

My body seemed to be telling me, "Chad, you should never work out again; you were not made for this." In the morning, however, inspired to get stronger, I decided to push through the pain and continue working out. Within a few months, I could bench-press more than double the weight than when I started, and I was no longer sore.

The same principle applies in the spirit realm. The more we exercise the gifts of the Spirit, the more breakthroughs we will see. Many of us have attempted to operate in healing, prophecy, or other gifts, but have quickly become discouraged because we did not see results after the first attempt. But because we are made in God's image and likeness, we all have the capacity to reflect His manifold gifts and glory.

Keep working out in the Spirit; you will never regret it.

POINTS TO PONDER

1. Bill Johnson often says, "We are not called to cultivate a theology based on our circumstances, but on the Word of God." What does he mean by this?

    ....

    ....

    ....

    ....

2. Do you tend to give up too soon when you are contending for a breakthrough? What was your most recent experience of this? Is it too late to try again?

    ....

    ....

    ....

    ....

3. Evaluate a significant breakthrough that has occurred in your life. See if you can trace the history of your faith efforts that led up to the breakthrough. What part did the faith and encouragement of others play? Did you have times of discouragement? How did you keep pressing forward?

    ....

    ....

    ....

    ....

MEDITATION

God wants you to pursue Him and to achieve the goals He sets before you. But He does not want you to become preoccupied with the achievements themselves. Your ultimate goal is to remain in Him and become closer to the Vine (see John 15:1-4).

Ask Him what that means for you right now, today. Does He want you to try something new? Or persist in trying something that has not yet succeeded? Or evaluate your "track record" with His help? Or simply rest and wait (which can be more difficult than taking action)? Don't stop asking Him until you know.

Chapter 9

HEAL THE BROKENHEARTED

Beni Johnson

Y OU DON'T HAVE TO go very far to see that many people need God's strength just to get through a day. They come in brokenness, looking for something to help them. Did you know that Jesus entrusted us to take His authority and release it onto others in need, to bring them into an encounter with the Most Holy One, and to let them see how much God loves them?

I once did a mini-study on Isaiah 61:1-9, and I found some interesting things. I had been doing some work with one of our pastors who helped people with very shattered pasts. Some of these people had been so shattered as small children that they had departmentalized their personalities out of a need for safety from abuse. They were truly shattered in their minds. We would pray and counsel with them and help them get to a place of safety so they could integrate back to a whole personality.

One day during this time, I was reading this passage in Isaiah, which is a prophetic word concerning Jesus. I started looking up the meaning of some of the words. Verse 1 reads, *"He has sent Me to heal the brokenhearted,"* which means "to bind up." I also found that the word *brokenhearted* means "shattered minds."[1] So this prophetic verse in Isaiah foretold Jesus coming to earth many years in the future with this as one of His assignments: to take those shattered in their minds and to bind them up as one would bind up a wound, to bring healing.

We also find in this passage that those who mourn are to be consoled and comforted and that they will be given beauty for their ashes, joy for their mourning, and a garment of praise for their heaviness (see Isa. 61:1-3). Then in verse 3 we see a change. God gives these people their identity. Those who have been shattered now become trees of righteousness that God Himself will plant for His glory: *"That they may be called trees of righteousness, the planting of the Lord, that He may be glorified."*

In verses 4-7, we see that God gives those who now have identity a destiny:

> *And they shall rebuild the old ruins, they shall raise up the former desolations, and they shall repair the ruined cities, the desolations of many generations. Strangers shall stand and feed your flocks, and the sons of the foreigner shall be your plowmen and your vinedressers. But you shall be named the priests of the Lord, they shall call you the servants of our God. You shall eat the riches of the Gentiles, and in their glory you shall boast. Instead of your shame you shall have double honor, and instead of confusion they shall rejoice in their portion. Therefore in their land they shall possess double; everlasting joy shall be theirs* (Isaiah 61:4-7).

Now we see how God has healed and restored, yet He has not only restored, but also made them able to become the people He created them to be and to do what He intended them to do. It's obvious what this passage is telling us: Those who come out of brokenness can and will come into a great destiny. They will take those things, those places that have been ruined and in desolation for many generations, and they will restore them. And, not only that, they will have lasting joy, everlasting joy!

It is like a huge dose of authority will be given to them. The devil tries to destroy us and keep us in our brokenness, and Jesus comes along and says, "Here, take Me. Let Me show you who you really are. Let Me show you your future."

I believe that when God sets you free from a disease of the body, soul, or spirit, you now have an authority to help others come into healing from that very thing you were delivered from. Many years ago, I was plagued with depression. I'm talking about the gut kind of depression that eats you up, the despair that attacks your inner being. When I was in my late teens, God delivered me from all depression in an instant. I was walking out of a bathroom and I cried out inside, "God, if You don't deliver me from this, I don't know what will happen to me." It was a very desperate cry for help. As I stepped through the door of the bathroom, I was set free. It lifted and has never returned after all these years. Now that's the way to get free! I wish it could be that way for all of us.

As I got older and matured in Christ, I found that an authority had been given to me to help others get free. When you see people who are ravished, shattered, and broken come into freedom, it is a grace and a beauty to behold. Then that free person steps into his or her anointing and destiny, and you watch that person take another broken person by the hand with compassion to bring freedom. That's the way of Love, and that's the way of our Father.

I have watched so many be set free and—best of all—fall in love with the Trinity through the simple act of having a heavenly encounter. I believe that God loves to show us His realm and is longing for us to see and feel what it is like to be with Him. Why not begin to experience His heavenly realm while we wait for His return or our own home-going?

POINTS TO PONDER

1. Read Isaiah 61:1-9 in its entirety. What verse or verses jump out at you with special meaning today? Why do you think the Spirit has highlighted them for you?

   ....

   ....

   ....

   ....

2. How has God brought you into freedom physically, emotionally, mentally, or spiritually? In what areas do you wish for further freedom?

   ....

   ....

   ....

   ....

3. Of course, freedom is a good thing, but what purpose does our freedom serve? Think about ways in which God's work in your life has enabled you to fulfill your destiny.

   ....

   ....

   ....

   ....

MEDITATION

God's desire and design is to meet us, heal us, and love us. He will do anything He can to accomplish that meeting. He longs for us more than we long for Him.

Open the shutters of your heart to Him once again, and let Him know how much you need Him. Ask Him to show you others who you could lead into the same freedoms that He has led you into.

ENDNOTE

1.   Brown, Driver, Briggs, and Gesenius, "The Old Testament Hebrew Lexicon," s.v. "Shabar"; http://www.searchgodsword.org/lex/heb/view.cgi?number=7665; accessed November 10, 2011; s.v. "Leb"; http://www.searchgodsword.org/lex/heb/view.cgi?number=01079; accessed November 30, 2011.

Chapter 10

ANGELS

Bill Johnson

W HEN GOD CHOSE TO beget the Messiah through the virgin Mary, He sent Gabriel the angel to bring the message. When the apostle Paul was about to suffer shipwreck, an angel of the Lord told him what would happen. On numerous occasions throughout the Scriptures, angels did what God could have done easily Himself. Why did God not do those things Himself? For the same reason He doesn't preach the Gospel: He has chosen to let those He has created enjoy the privilege of service in His Kingdom.

God created humankind, and He created angelic beings. Angels are impressive beings. They are glorious and powerful—so much so that when they showed up in the Scriptures, people often fell down to worship them. While it is foolish to worship our fellow creatures, it is equally foolish to ignore them. Angels are assigned to serve wherever we serve, *if the supernatural element is needed.* We read in Hebrews 1:14 that the angels are ministering spirits sent to serve those who will inherit the Kingdom—which means you and me.

I believe angels have been often bored because we live the kind of lifestyles that don't require much of their help. Their assignment is to assist us in supernatural endeavors. If we do not take the necessary risks to undertake supernatural endeavors, then there is little room for the supernatural. Faith-filled risk-taking releases solutions to impossible situations. John Wimber said, "Faith is spelled R-I-S-K."

When the Church regains its appetite for the impossible, the angels will increase their activities among people. As the fires of revival intensify, so do the supernatural activities around us. If angels are assigned to assist us in supernatural endeavors, then there must be need for their help. I challenge you to pursue God passionately and, in your pursuit, to insist on a supernatural lifestyle—one that keeps the hosts of Heaven busy ushering in the King and His Kingdom.

Now, while God has provided angels to assist us in our commission, I don't take the posture that we are to command them. Some people feel they have that liberty. I, however, believe it is a dangerous proposition. Scripturally, we have reason to believe that angels are to be commissioned by God Himself in response to our prayers.

Daniel needed an answer from God. He prayed for 21 days. An angel finally showed up with his answer. He said to Daniel,

> *"Do not fear, Daniel, for from the first day that you set your heart to understand, and to humble yourself before your God, your words were heard; and I have come because of your words. But the prince of the kingdom of Persia withstood me twenty-one days; and behold, Michael, one of the chief princes, came to help me, for I had been left alone there with the kings of Persia"* (Daniel 10:12-13).

When Daniel prayed, God responded by sending an angel with the answer. The angel ran into interference. Daniel continued to pray, which appears to have helped to release the archangel Michael to fight and release the first angel to deliver the message. This is only one biblical instance of many in which God commanded angels to come in response to the prayers of the saints.

Angels respond to God's command, and they enforce His Word. But the voice of His word is also heard when the Father speaks to the hearts of His people. Angels await the people of God speaking His Word. I believe angels pick up the fragrance of the throne room through the word spoken by people. They can tell when a word has its origins in the heart of the Father. In turn, they recognize that word as their assignment.

I saw this happen once at a meeting in Germany. Before the meeting, I had been praying with some of the leaders who were sponsoring the meetings. As we were praying, I saw a brief picture in my mind of a woman sitting to my right with an arthritic spine. It was the visual equivalent of the "still small voice"—as easy to miss as it is to get. In this picture, I had her stand, and I declared over her, "The Lord Jesus heals you!"

When it came time for the meeting, I asked if anyone was there who had arthritis in the spine. A woman to my right waved her hand. I had her stand up and declared over her, "The Lord Jesus heals you!" Then I asked her where her pain was. She wept as she said, "It is impossible, but it is gone!"

I believe that angels enforced a word that originated in the heart of the Father. For that moment, I was the voice of His word.

POINTS TO PONDER

1. Sometimes it's good to remember that angels are working behind the scenes. Think of a time when God's power broke into your life or the life of another person. How do you think angels may have been involved? How do you think you or the other person helped bring about the outcome? How do you suspect that "co-laboring" worked in that situation?

   ....

   ....

   ....

   ....

2. Have you ever sensed angels? If so, how could you tell that angels were present? Can a person always tell the difference between an angelic presence and God's presence?

   ....

   ....

   ....

   ....

3. How can you do your part to keep the angels who get assigned to help you serve God from being "bored"?

   ....

   ....

   ....

   ....

MEDITATION

Angels are stronger, more beautiful, and much more powerful than people are. God created them before He created human beings. Angels are immortal (see Matt. 22:30). As spirits, angels are not restricted by bodies as we are, and they are not restricted by time and space.

They are not omniscient (all-knowing), omnipotent (all-powerful), or omnipresent as God is, but they know a lot more than we do and convey a lot more of God's power than we do. In fact, much of our experience of God's glorious, powerful presence is revealed to us by His angels.

While not mistakenly worshiping angels, you should remind yourself about them on a regular basis. They co-labor with you and with the Church worldwide, bringing the rule and reign of God to this planet. Search out some of the scriptural references to angels and ask God to keep you mindful of their availability and their role.

Chapter 11

RESONATING WITH JESUS' JOY

Paul Manwaring

WE ARE STILL TRYING to wrap our minds around the idea that our salvation was not just about God forgiving our sin. So it's difficult to imagine that both bringing us into His family and bringing us close to Him would bring God so much joy that He would gladly endure the horror of the cross. But the very substance of God is that He is a Father who delights in His children and who created His children to delight in Him. In creating us as His children for His glory, He created us for joy. Thus the Westminster Catechism superbly states: "Man's chief end is to glorify God, and to enjoy him forever."

This makes me think of a tuning fork that vibrates when its note is sounded. When God is before us, when we are close to Him, we resonate with the same sound that is God. We rejoice in His presence, for in His *presence is fullness of joy*" (Ps. 16:11). Our glory rejoices—the substance that we share with God is expressed in the intimacy and exchange of being with Him as Father and children, and that expression is joy.

In his book, *Orthodoxy*, G.K. Chesterton said, "Man is more himself, man is more manlike, when joy is the fundamental thing in him, and grief the superficial."[1] And C.S. Lewis said, "Joy is the serious business of heaven."[2] God's purpose in restoring us as sons and daughters and bringing us close to Himself is nothing less than to bring us into joy. I submit that the level of joy in a person, a family, a city, a nation, and the world is the direct measure of how fully they have stepped into the knowledge and reality of the glory of God. Certainly, if His presence is fullness of joy, then our level of joy reveals the degree to which we have learned to live in His presence.

Jesus had much to say about joy in His final words to His disciples before He went to the cross. He instructed them to abide in His love and His commands, explaining, *"These things I have spoken to you, that My joy may remain in you, and that your joy may be full"* (John 15:11). He promised that, though they would grieve for a time when He had gone, *"I will see you again and your heart will rejoice, and your joy no one will take from you"* (John 16:22). But then He laid out the great, heavenly blank check:

> *In that day you will ask Me nothing. Most assuredly, I say to you, whatever you ask the Father in My name He will give you. Until now you have asked nothing in My name. Ask, and you will receive, that your joy may be full* (John 16:23-24).

Asking our Father for things in Christ's name is arguably the activity par excellence by which we walk in sonship. True sons and daughters ask their Father for things and receive them. And we can always identify whether our asking and receiving are genuine by looking at their fruit. When we truly enter into asking and receiving from our Father, the unmistakable result is fullness of joy.

After instructing His disciples to ask, Jesus showed them in His high priestly prayer where to start asking (see John 17). Some of us worry about whether we really know how to ask the Father for things in Jesus' name, whether we're praying in His will. But we simply can't go wrong if we ask for the same things for which Jesus asked, especially by asking for the thing that was uppermost in His mind and heart as He laid down

His life for us. His greatest request and desire was that we be perfected in unity with Him and each other through His glory (see John 17:23). This request is to be the bedrock of our lives, for all of our asking and all of our living must flow from our constant pursuit to be one with Him and each other in every aspect of our being.

Jesus made it clear that this oneness would bring the world to faith:

> *I do not pray for these alone, but also for those who will believe in Me through their word; that they all may be one, as You, Father, are in Me, and I in You; that they also may be one in Us, that the world may believe that You sent Me* (John 17:20-21).

Here Jesus added to His outline of faith. Before He came, Moses and the prophets were the key to recognizing Him for who He really is. But now that He has been glorified, He is to be recognized through His brothers and sisters. It is when our lives "tremble" with the extreme joy of living in the presence of our Father and walking as His sons and daughters that the world will recognize Christ as the One who came to restore them to the purpose for which they were created—glory.

POINTS TO PONDER

1. What is joy? Is it always accompanied with a delighted grin? How did Jesus show His joy? How many ways can you think of to express it?

   ....

   ....

   ....

   ....

2. Do you think you have missed joy at times? What happened? In many cases, you can choose to revisit a circumstance and respond in a different way so as to share Jesus' joy.

   ....

   ....

   ....

   ....

3. Is joy a solo experience? What is it about joy that impels relationship?

   ....

   ....

   ....

   ....

MEDITATION

Joy cannot be held as a theoretical value; it must be experienced personally to be valid. And yet you cannot engineer it for yourself. You cannot commandeer it. It is a gift, the byproduct of your response to an invitation from God Himself.

Open your heart to Him anew. Offer yourself to Him. Listen. Do you hear His still, small voice? What is He telling you? Even one of His words is enough to ignite joy in your heart.

ENDNOTES

1.   G.K. Chesterton, *Orthodoxy* (New York: John Lane Company, 1908), 296.

2.   C.S. Lewis, *Letters to Malcolm* (New York: Harcourt, Inc., 1964), 93.

Chapter 12

HE GETS TO DO SOMETHING

Kevin Dedmon

I N GOD'S SOVEREIGNTY, He has determined that He will speak through us and work through our hands here on the earth. As ambassadors of Christ, we are His mouthpieces, and we are His hands extended.

Certainly, it is *"Christ in [us], the hope of glory"* (Col. 1:27). And the Christ *in* us is just waiting to be the Christ *through* us, because He wants to become the hope of glory for others around us. He wants to intervene in the lives of many other people, and it is our risk that unties His hands and unleashes His voice to release the miraculous works that the people of the earth so desperately need.

The apostle James promised that *"the prayer of faith will save the sick, and the Lord will raise him up"* (James 5:14-15). God is just waiting for us to trust that He will intervene in our lives and in the lives of others. Risk makes us take action and proves that we truly believe.

Did you know that God is pleased with the fact that our risk-taking affords Him the opportunity to intervene in our lives and circumstances? He is pleased because He gets to do something! In a sense, when we take risk we relieve God and the angels of Heaven from boredom. God has been waiting for us to pursue the impossible so that He can work on our behalf.

In Hebrews 11:6, we are told that, *"without faith, it is impossible to please Him...."* Notice that it is not our performance or success that pleases God. Rather, *it is faith expressed in risk that pleases God.* Even when we take a risk and give a wrong word of knowledge, God is pleased. We cannot change His mind about loving us.

In this venture of stepping out in risk, it is important to note that our intrinsic value and position as His children does not become greater with more risk-taking—He is already fully pleased with us. The Father was already fully pleased with Jesus before He took the risk to turn water into wine, pray for someone, or walk on water. At Jesus' baptism, before He had performed any miracles, the Father said, *"This is My beloved Son, in whom I am well pleased"* (Matt. 3:17). In the same way, God is already pleased with us because we are His children. We cannot do one thing to earn any more of His pleasure toward us.

In the parable of the persistent widow, Jesus concludes with the question, *"When the Son of Man comes, will He really find faith on the earth?"* (Luke 18:8). In other words, will He find that we and others have kept taking risks of faith until Jesus returns? The apostle Paul exhorts, *"Examine yourselves as to whether you are in the faith. Test yourselves. Do you not know yourselves, that Jesus Christ is in you?..."* (2 Cor. 13:5). Risk is not to be merely a one-time event, but rather a complete lifestyle.

Understandably, taking risk does not come naturally. It must be pursued intentionally as a first option. Risk requires a commitment to continually pursue the impossible. Even accomplished risk-takers know that every time they take a real risk, their hearts are beating out of their chests. You may never get used to taking risk, but the more you step into it, the more normal it will become. Create a culture of risk in your own life by venturing prayerfully into impossible territory again and again.

POINTS TO PONDER

1. Do you think that risk-taking is only for certain kinds of people (and that you, perhaps, are not one of them)? Think of the various personalities of the apostles and leaders of the early Church. While the risks they took may have varied, do you think that every one of them lived as part of a culture of risk-taking? What were some of the miracles that occurred as a direct result of their faith?

   ....

   ....

   ....

   ....

2. How long has it been since you have stepped out in risk? Can you say that you "have a testimony" of risk-taking faith? What is holding you back from making huge investments in supernatural ventures? What is preventing you from going after the most impossible dreams?

   ....

   ....

   ....

   ....

3. What unexpected faith venture will you step into today? Tomorrow?

   ....

   ....

   ....

   ....

MEDITATION

In cultivating a supernatural culture of risk, we must be willing to try for the impossible even though we may miss the mark at times. In going after our supernatural destiny, we must be willing to make our situation worse. We must take a chance on the small openings in life. We may not get it right every time, but if we do not try to do the miraculous works of Jesus, we will miss a good part of our supernatural destiny.

For the Christian, risk is intended to characterize a culture, not to be only a one-time event. You cannot say to yourself, "OK, I stepped out in risk. I'm glad I got that requirement out of the way. Now I can go back to a safe life." No, risk——cultivated and repeated over time——is meant to be a major part of a Kingdom lifestyle. A single risk is good only for the one time it is used, so you need to take risks repeatedly.

As you apply the risk factor and step into your supernatural destiny, God will empower you to go to the next levels of supernatural break-through. I release to you an impartation of grace to live a radical lifestyle of radical risk!

Chapter 13

FAITH IS SPELLED R-I-S-K

Chris Overstreet

FAITH IS SPELLED: R-I-S-K, with love and honor.

Honor places a high worth on every person God has created, regardless of his or her social status or spiritual condition. Honor raises people up to the high calling that Jesus has for them. We honor people not for what we can get from them, but because we have been honored (raised up) by Jesus. We don't honor people for who they appear to be. We honor them for who Jesus says they are:

> *Having your conduct honorable among the Gentiles, that when they speak against you as evildoers, they may, by your good works which they observe, glorify God in the day of visitation* (1 Peter 2:12).

Years ago, I chased down a person in a power wheelchair because I wanted to see this man healed. After I asked him if I could pray for him, he resisted me. In spite of his resistance, I kept trying to force him to receive prayer. What I didn't realize at the time was that I was not valuing or honoring him as a person. In that moment, he was nothing more than a project to me. The Lord taught me through this situation that regardless of someone's physical condition, that person still deserves to be honored as a person.

Can you honor someone you don't agree with? There have been many situations where I've been placed in a conversation where I didn't agree with the other person's opinion. But because Jesus honors this person, I am still required to honor and love that person. As believers, we should honor people regardless of whether we agree with them or not. It's not helpful to be disrespectful when presenting the Gospel to others. Our responsibility is to love and honor others all the time.

I disrupted a whole restaurant once by standing up and preaching. The problem was not that I was preaching, but that I was not honoring the restaurant and the customers who were eating there. The owner of the restaurant was not impressed with my ability to preach, and he didn't ask me to come back. I should have used common sense and basic wisdom to understand that I was a disruption rather than a blessing.

Honoring people must come from a genuine heart of love regardless of what people look like, smell like, or act like. It also entails honoring your environment. You can be bold, but at the same time, you need to honor businesses and people around you. Use wisdom while ministering in business settings. One of your values should be to see businesses prosper.

In 1999, I was hearing stories of people hearing God and responding to what God was saying. Some people told stories of how God would direct them to go to a certain location and they would meet a certain person that God spoke to them about. Could God use me like that? Could it really be possible? Soon after, in prayer, I asked God, "Speak to me, Lord. I'll do anything You tell me to do." And I felt like He told me to go to a certain location in the city, where I would find an individual on a certain street. I was so pumped up! It was my time to shine! So I gathered a couple of my friends and we headed out late that evening to follow the voice of God.

As we made our way into the city, I started to feel uneasy in my heart. We were not able to find the location that I thought the Lord had directed me to. To top it off, there was no person there. We pulled over in the car, and I started to get upset. I was upset at myself, and I was thinking in my mind—*I knew it. This stuff is not for me. Supernatural evangelism is only for special and gifted people. After all, I have a past. Why would God want to use someone like me, after everything I've done in the past?* I started to cry, and my friends in the vehicle tried to cheer me up.

My friend Laura said to me, "Chris, you did not miss it tonight."

I responded, "What are you talking about? We couldn't find the place, and we couldn't find the person."

She insisted, "Chris—you didn't miss it tonight." She went on to tell me that most people would do nothing with what they felt like the Lord showed them. Then she proceeded to tell me, "God is looking at your heart, Chris, and He loves your heart, because you have a heart of love and you are willing to take a risk for Him."

That day I learned a valuable lesson. When my heart is motivated to love God and to follow His leading and to love people, I will never miss it. It takes time to learn how to walk, like a child. A little child takes a couple of steps, then falls down. But eventually, that child learns how to walk. Each of us are born again to become children of God, and we are all learning how to walk this thing out with a Father who loves us and is proud of us when we take steps that require risk.

POINTS TO PONDER

1. Has your faith-walk with God involved public risk-taking? How has it worked out? What have you learned?

    ....

    ....

    ....

    ....

2. Testimonies inspire us to take similar risks of faith. Explore the subtle difference between following through on true inspiration from God and our human tendency to create our own testimony and thereby earn status with fellow believers. Will God sometimes use us regardless of our mixed motives? Why will He let us fail sometimes?

    ....

    ....

    ....

    ....

MEDITATION

You can stay safe—and wonder why God never uses you in the ways He uses others—or you can decide to take your first wobbly steps of faith and see where He takes you. When you make faith a core value in your life, and adopt a lifestyle of risk-taking, that's when you will become more aware of the Kingdom opportunities around you.

Ask Him to help you stand up and put your weight on your feet of faith. He will help you get back up when you lose your balance and fall. He will teach you how to love and honor other people. He will train your senses—including your common sense—so that you can walk with confidence.

Chapter 14

WHAT IS NORMAL?

Danny Silk

I HATE SNAKES! I HAVE killed a fair number of snakes simply because I believe they are dangerous. A friend was visiting us not too long ago, and he told me about hiking with his family and coming across a rattlesnake that someone (like me) had killed alongside the trail. My friend's son was distraught that someone could do such a thing. He cried out, "*Dad!* They killed it! Why would anyone do such a thing? Dad, why would anyone kill a snake?" I was silent during the story. His son was sitting right there while my friend told me how their whole family was grieved over this incident. I was stunned. I'd never before met anyone who *loved* snakes. All my *normal* friends think like me; they hate snakes, too. My belief about snakes was being confronted.

What's normal? We get our idea of normal from our families, from the people who have had the most direct influence over us in our formative years. Sometimes the first time we recognize that our "normal" is not typical is when we leave our families to get married. "What? You've never had ketchup on your tacos? I thought everyone ate tacos that way." We look at our spouse's family and think, "Your family is weird." Our spouse is thinking the same thing.

We don't know what we really believe because we have believed it for so long, since long before we developed the ability to separate true from false. You can say to your children, "Tonight a man in a red and white suit is going to land on our roof, slide down the chimney (that we don't have), and leave presents for you. We are putting cookies and milk out for him." The kids wake up in the morning, and say, "Wow! Presents! There's a bite out of the cookie! It's all true!"

"Yes, and next a bunny rabbit is going to bounce around the world and hide eggs all over the house. He's also going to leave you a basket with chocolate in it." Sure enough in the morning, there are the eggs and the basket. It's true! (We go on to explain that when their teeth fall out from eating the candy, a fairy will swap their teeth for cash if they put them under their pillow....)

Children don't have the ability to say, "This just feels wrong," or "You're full of baloney, Dad." A five-year-old won't know truth from deception. The child trusts his or her environment to develop a grasp of truth.

And sooner or later, the child learns the power game. In order to survive in a shifting environment, people try to control each other's beliefs. Taking the information they possess, they try to gain the advantage.

Author Steven Covey tells of riding in a subway car, exhausted from a long day of work, enjoying his peaceful ride home. The subway stopped and the door opened to admit a man and his four children. The children began to amuse themselves by running from one end of the car to the other, screaming. Covey grew increasingly frustrated by how this father was allowing his offspring to run wild, seemingly oblivious to their behavior. Eventually, one of the children stumbled over an elderly lady who yelped, and Covey had finally had enough. He jumped up, walked over to the father, and said, "Hey! Don't you see what your children are doing?"

The man looked up in sort of a daze and replied, "Oh, I'm sorry. We're returning from the hospital. Their mother just died. I am sure they don't know what to do."

Stunned by the information, Covey said, "Oh, I am so sorry. Stay right there. Let me help you with your children." He had gone from angry to helpful in an instant. Why? Because he got some new information. What he had believed to be true about the situation changed. The behaviors that had come from his belief system changed, too.

The fruit of the presence of God in our lives is self-control—not control of others. And our motivation to exercise self-control improves in direct proportion to our trust in God. When we find our security in God, we have no need to try to mold the people around us to match our belief system. Paul said, *"The fruit of the Spirit is love, joy, peace, longsuffering, kindness, goodness, faithfulness, gentleness, self-control. Against such there is no law"* (Gal. 5:22-23).

When we choose to exercise that power of self-control toward loving God, our spouses, our children, and the people around us, we are partnering with the Holy Spirit and inviting His Kingdom to reign in our homes. But when we partner with a spirit of fear, we invite the kingdom of intimidation, manipulation, and anger to reign.

The spiritual environment around us boils down to the presence of either fear or love. Which "normal" do you want?

POINTS TO PONDER

1. Have you ever discovered that what you thought you believed to be true was not consistent with how you actually responded to a situation, particularly when you experienced a strong emotion such as fear or anger? What did you learn about your beliefs through that experience?

....

....

....

....

2. People can exercise a lot of wit and discipline in their effort to stay in line and avoid censure from others. How is this different from the supernatural fruit of self-control?

....

....

....

....

3. What are the keys to "normal" in the Kingdom of God? How can you recognize them?

....

....

....

....

MEDITATION

The Holy Spirit is the Spirit of true power. Human anger and violence, subterfuge and lies are false powers that people use to control others. Living as we do within the clash of two kingdoms—the Kingdom of God and the kingdom of this world—the kind of power we choose in a given situation depends on our belief system, our allegiance to the specific beliefs that we hold true.

Offer your belief system to God in prayer, asking Him to revise it where necessary and to help you to "get it" where His truth is concerned.

Chapter 15

NO FEAR ZONE

Beni Johnson

WHEN OUR THIRD GRANDCHILD, Haley, was born, her mommy, Jenn, had an infection, and the doctor had to perform an emergency C-section. As they brought the baby out of surgery and rushed her into NICU, they told us that Haley wasn't responding well. They perform a test called the Apgar score on babies when they are first born. It has a numerical score, with ten being the best. Haley's score was two. We found out later that babies who have a score of two usually don't make it. When they gave us this news, we as a family had to make a decision. Would we agree with this bad news? I will never forget that feeling. This was our son's firstborn. Everything was so new and exciting; then we got this bad report. I remember going and sitting in a chair in the waiting room. I put my face in my hands and asked God what was going on. I heard these words, "It's just warfare. Say 'no!'" So that's what I did. The whole family prayed. This was not to happen. Within ten minutes, the nurse came out and told us that Haley's Apgar was up to seven and that she would be fine. As I write this, Haley is very alive and well, changing the world around her for Jesus.

Fear has a way of coming up and biting you. Everything seems to be going great in your life and you are walking in peace. All of a sudden, there fear is, trying to envelope you, trying to destroy your peace. We as believers have to make a choice to resist fear. We as a family had to make a choice that we would not partner with fear. The devil has legal rights only if we agree with him. The tool he uses to get us is fear. He does not play fair with us. He will go right for our soft spots.

The Bible urges us not to be afraid:

> *Do not be afraid of sudden terror* [the NASB uses "sudden fear"], *nor of trouble from the wicked when it comes; for the Lord will be your confidence, and will keep your foot from being caught* (Proverbs 3:25-26).

At Bethel Church, my job is to oversee the prayer. As the prayer pastor, I get a lot of emails from all over the world. Many of the emails are asking for emergency prayer, and they come with a high prayer alert. Many of them are good and appropriate, but others are so full of fear that I must reject the spirit that is attached to them. I refuse to pray out of fear.

What I *will* do is just stop and ask God how to pray about the crisis and wait for His direction. I must stay focused on God and not on the crisis. When you move your prayers into fear, you can't possibly get a clear handle on how to pray according to how Heaven is praying. All you can hear is the heartbeat of fear. We must be like the sons of Issachar (see 1 Chron. 12:32); we must understand and know what to do. Staying focused and keeping to Heaven's plan is the most important thing of all.

Do you ever just sit back and think about the world, what it looks like now, and what is really going on? Why are world events happening? What is really making those events happen? What is the root? Not just on the surface, but deeper—what is making things go the way they are going?

When I look at the world, I can recognize the devil's plan. The root is fear. It really is a simple plan. All the devil has to do is make sure that we walk in fear; then all of our responses will be out of the place of fear. The most repeated command in the Bible is "Do not fear." From Genesis to Revelation, God has repeatedly told us not to fear. God knows our humanness, and He knows we need Him.

So when I sit back and look at the world and see what God is doing, it makes me happy. Do these words sound familiar?—*"For I know the thoughts that I think toward you, says the Lord, thoughts of peace and not of evil, to give you a future and a hope"* (Jer. 29:11).

Declare that you will be a "no fear zone" and that you will bring a spirit of faith-filled confidence everywhere you go!

POINTS TO PONDER

1. Are you a naturally fearful person? What do you tend to do when something frightening intrudes on your life? If God has helped you overcome your fears, how has He done it?

....

....

....

....

2. Think of a time when you trusted God instead of floundering in fear. Did it take you some time to really trust? Whether it took a long or a short time, what was the outcome of your fear-free faith?

....

....

....

....

3. We are urged not to be afraid of circumstances, but on the other hand we are supposed to "fear" God. How is our human fear (of pain, difficulty, suffering) different from a holy fear of God?

....

....

....

....

MEDITATION

The Old Testament is filled with great stories of kings and leaders of Israel who looked to God for wisdom. Their only hope and salvation was their dependence on what God would do. The people of the New Testament carried this dependence on God to a new level because all of the believers were filled with the Holy Spirit.

Talk to your Father God about something fearful that you are facing right now. Make it your full intention to trust Him with all your heart and mind. Then take note of what He tells you to do.

Chapter 16

Taking Captive Every Scary Thought

Chad Dedmon

I N 2002, I ATTENDED the Bethel School of Supernatural Ministry. Frequently we practiced hearing from the Lord in order to increase in accuracy and grow in our intimacy with Jesus. What we learned inside the four walls of our school, we took outside of the classroom as we stepped out and began to exercise our faith.

When my classmates and I went out to eat, each of us made it a point to get a prophetic word for our server. This could include everything from prophetic words of encouragement, something simple that connects people to the heart of their heavenly Father, to words of knowledge. As the word gets more specific, the level of risk in the delivery of the word increases.

On one occasion, I kept hearing the phrase, "I like my little brown house." I also heard the name "Vicki," so I glanced at the server's nametag to check if it said Vicki. It didn't. I asked God for clarification, but I wasn't getting any.

Meanwhile, my friends started to give her words of encouragement. Honestly, at this point, I just wanted to have a simple word to give her from God. I was scared that if I gave her what I had gotten, she would think that I was a spiritual "fruit loop."

My turn came. So, I went for it and asked her, "Does the name Vicki mean anything to you?" My legs were shaking under the table because I was so nervous. She took a step back and said, "Wow, that is my middle name!"

Encouraged, I gave the second word. I explained to her that I kept hearing the phrase, "I like my little brown house." Immediately, she put her tray down on the table, and in an intense tone of voice asked if I had been talking to her husband. I replied, "No, I don't know your husband." She explained that she and her husband had been discussing selling their house. That very morning, she had been saying the phrase to him, "I like my little brown house." She asked me how I could possibly have known about that conversation. I told her I didn't know, but God did, and He cared about every area of her life.

Then I asked her if she had any pain in her body at the moment. She told me she actually did have pain in her lower back from a car accident ten years earlier. We all prayed for her back, and the pain left. I was glad I had taken the risk to tell her what I had heard from God on her behalf.

You see, you can receive information from God about others that will not make any sense to you. Don't get introspective about it. It usually won't make sense to you because it doesn't apply to you. However, it will often make sense to the person receiving the word.

Later that night, I contemplated what had happened at the restaurant and how extremely nervous I was before I delivered the word to the server. I had received accurate information from God about her life, but was so scared to tell it to her. Why was I so scared to do the very thing I am called to do—encourage people with the word of God?

I asked myself, "When I see people in a wheelchair in public, and I have a desire to pray for them, why does fear consume me?" Why would I be scared of approaching a harmless person in a wheelchair, asking "Do you want to be healed?" and praying for a touch of God's healing presence—especially since the person may jump out of the wheelchair and begin to praise Jesus? What can possibly be scary about that?

According to Second Corinthians 10:5, we need to learn how to take every thought captive to the obedience of Christ. The spirit of unbelief can speak in the form of our personal thoughts. For example, *What if this doesn't work? What if this person doesn't get healed when I pray?* These thoughts arise from the fear that we will fail and also from the fear of people.

Interestingly, I still feel apprehensive many times before praying for someone in public. When I feel fear, I know that the enemy is present, trying to keep me from stepping into my destiny in that moment.

I remember as a boy growing up in the church, people would tell me, "When the enemy reveals himself in a situation, it is usually because it is the last card that he can play." With that in mind, I can use fear like a thermometer to gauge what God is about to do. Whenever the enemy tries to shut me down with accusations of intimidation and fear, I take courage because I know my destiny in God is about to be revealed.

POINTS TO PONDER

1. Have you ever taken time to evaluate your fears, specifically your fears about stepping out in faith to deliver a word to someone? What is your worst fear? How can you counter it?

   ....

   ....

   ....

   ....

2. Many heroes of the faith struggled with fear before they stepped into their breakthrough. When God commissioned Joshua to take the people into the Promised Land, He had to tell him three times to be strong and courageous. (See Joshua 1:5-7,9.) Did Joshua take God seriously? Did He operate out of faith rather than fear? How do you know?

   ....

   ....

   ....

   ....

MEDITATION

You must choose to conquer your fears and not let fear dictate your decisions. However, once fear is overcome, that doesn't necessarily guarantee that you'll never have to deal with it again. Fear can continue to show up at your doorstep, but you can choose whether or not you will open the door and welcome it in. Every time you resist the inclination to submit to fear, you build your spiritual muscles to be able to resist fear and embrace faith.

What are you afraid of today? Take your scary thoughts captive and present them before God. Actively choose to put your trust in Him. Say out loud: *"I will trust and not be afraid..."* (Isa. 12:2).

Chapter 17

A SETUP FOR SUCCESS

Bill Johnson

GOD NEVER FAILS TO give you the tools you need before you need them. He will keep you away from challenges that you are not yet prepared to face. The corollary truth is that the battles and tests into which He will take you will be the ones for which He has prepared you. God is a good Father, and He never sets us up to fail, but only to grow.

I believe that the reason many believers fall into the trap of fear and anxiety in the midst of crisis is because they allow the enemy to distract them from the fact that they are prepared with weapons they already have in their arsenal. It's easy for us to feel blindsided by events that we did not expect, but nothing surprises God, which is why He prepares us for what's ahead. Remembering that He has seen ahead and has prepared us makes a huge difference in our response to difficulty.

With our hearts anchored in this truth about His nature, we will be oriented to take inventory of our tools and weapons and start using them when we come up against a challenge. The bedrock of an automatic response from us is the burning conviction that God is good, always good!

Doubting His goodness, making up explanations for things we don't understand (the source of a lot of bad theology), or falling into anxiety and disappointment will no longer be options for us. It's like knowing exactly what to do when the oil light goes on in your car. When the truth of God's goodness is *not* firmly anchored in your heart, you are not only dislodged from your purpose in conflict, you also do not possess the sensitivity of heart or the faith to perceive the tools God has given you in preparation for an upcoming challenge.

We learn this lesson from Jesus' disciples. Shortly after they witnessed the miracle of the loaves and fishes, the disciples were in a boat in the middle of a storm on the lake. In the midst of the storm, Jesus walked out on the water to them and stilled the storm. The disciples were overwhelmed by His demonstration of power, their own unbelief, and probably their corresponding lack of readiness to face another obstacle in their own authority.

Mark gave the following explanation for their reaction: *"For they had not understood about the loaves, because their heart was hardened"* (Mark 6:52). In this season of His ministry, Jesus was training His disciples to do what He did. Every miracle He did in their presence was a lesson about the nature of God and an invitation for them to live from that revelation. In calming the storm, He was demonstrating a dimension of God's power and authority that logically connected to the power and authority He had demonstrated earlier in the miracle of the loaves. It's as if He taught them multiplication and was now moving on to algebra. But they couldn't move on, because they failed to understand the first lesson.

Why didn't they get the lesson of the loaves? Their hearts were hard. They lacked the basic faith in who God is, and they lacked an understanding of the way He was working to orient them to learn the lessons He was teaching to prepare them for life and ministry. How sobering it must have been to see that it is possible to be perfectly obedient to the Lord's commands (in obtaining the available food and in handing it out to the multitudes), to participate fully in a miracle—and still not understand, because of a hard heart, the tools that God was handing them. Jesus' rebuke gave them a chance to repent, in order to recover what they had missed in the miracle.

Our ability to connect with what God is doing in the midst of difficult circumstances depends on our ability to remember who He is and what He has done in our lives—our relational history with Him. I guarantee that if you are currently facing a situation that seems to be beyond your strength or understanding, and if you take some time to rehearse your history with the Lord over the past year or so, you will always find a tool—for example, a prophetic word, a Scripture verse that has leapt out at you, a testimony, or a prayer strategy—that God has already put into your arsenal, something that provides a key to overcoming the present situation. You might also need to repent for any hardness of heart that has kept you from getting what He has made available to you. Your perception of which forces are the most operative in your life will shift. That perception will open you up to the lessons about the unseen realities all around you. Such a shift makes learning natural.

POINTS TO PONDER

1. What is the effect of having a hardened heart? What must a person substitute for a hardened heart upon recognizing it and repenting for it?

    ....

    ....

    ....

    ....

2. Can you identify a circumstance in which you had (or perhaps still have) a hardened heart? How has it kept you from succeeding against a challenge? What can you do about it?

    ....

    ....

    ....

    ....

MEDITATION

God sent the Israelites to Egypt so He could pick a fight. He blessed and multiplied His people until they were a threat to the enemy; then He hardened the hearts of the Egyptians and provoked them. This divine setup justified His rising up on behalf of His people, displaying His wonders, pouring out plagues on the Egyptians, and bringing the Israelites out loaded with spoils. What a strategy!

God not only sets up a conflict and prepares you for it, but He leads you straight into it. Your success over the conflict depends upon your grasp of the essentials: His overarching goodness and His careful, individualized attention to equip you for whatever He leads you into. Assent to whatever He's sending you into next. Expect great things!

Chapter 18

FEAR VS. LOVE

Danny Silk

GOD PUT THESE LITTLE glands inside our brains called amygdalae, almond-shaped structures located deep within the temporal lobes of our brains. These glands help determine emotional responses, especially those associated with fear. When something threatening or unexpected occurs in your environment, your amygdalae kick on and begin to flood your body with these messages: *React. Defend. Disappear. Fight. Flee.*

It doesn't take a rocket scientist to discover that people who are scared are not at their creative best. If you've ever been near a person who is drowning and panicking, then you know it is a good idea to keep your distance. Throw a rope or extend a pole, but do not let that person grab hold of you or you will become a buoy. Oh sure, the person will apologize later, if you survive. But scared people are not thinking about the team, family, church, or anyone else besides themselves. Fear is a dangerous element for humans to navigate through. Most do not manage it well.

Each one of us creates an atmosphere, a reality, around us. But we can only reproduce on the outside that which is on the inside. If our thoughts and affections are wrapped up with a spirit of fear, while we may think we are smoothly hiding it, we cannot mask the anxiety we have allowed into our lives. This is worst of all in a family or a church when the parents or leaders end up affecting the measure of security that the children or people feel. Fearful and uptight leaders produce fearful and uptight people.

Fear and love are mortal enemies. They cannot occupy the same space. Fear and love are like darkness and light, salt water and fresh water, cursing and blessing. When they are both present, one of them has to win.

God is love and His perfect love casts out fear (see 1 John 4:8,18). Not only does love cast out fear, but it brings security and safety and *shalom*. Fear departs. Safety prevails. Freedom grows.

If leaders understand that their top priority is to make the house of God a safe place, then as people encounter the safe place of God's covenant in their lives, their potential, their anointings, and their creativity start to rise to the surface and find room to be manifested in the house. Beyond that, if people can feel secure and free to be who God created them to be, then they will be able to influence the world with the Kingdom of Heaven.

Of course, as you probably are aware, high levels of freedom can generate conflict, because other people express themselves in ways that activate our amygdalae. Unless we have developed a core value of honor (one of the expressions of love), we will find that our discomfort around those who make us afraid tends to make us shut down their freedom. It is typical, for example, when a teenager begins to explore his or her freedom, for the parents to become afraid. The further the child moves from how the parents live, the more likely the parents are to step in and shut down the child's choices. The result is conflict. But when both the parents and the teenager practice honor, which contains within it love and trust, fear will be prevented from ruling their decisions.

From the way we dress to the style of music we listen to, to whether we drink alcohol or not, to whether we speak English or Christianese, to whether the gifts of the Spirit are in operation today or not, the reality is that freedom is going to bring our differences to the surface and cause friction within a community. When our paradigms get upset, our amygdalae get jacked up—and we often end up showing others our worst behavior.

The question is whether we will learn to use honor to navigate through the conflict when it arises. Conflict is not inherently evil. As a matter of fact, when conflict goes away, *life* most likely leaves with it. Sometimes we think that peace means the absence of conflict, but true peace is always the result of victory. And I cannot think of a victory that did not first begin with a struggle.

POINTS TO PONDER

1. Do you consider yourself to be "conflict-avoidant"? Whether or not you do, have you ever considered conflict in this light before? What immediate application can you give to what you have just learned by reading about fear and love?

   ....

   ....

   ....

   ....

2. How have you seen true love (with honor and trust) modeled in your family or church? How have you seen it replace fear? Remember, fear can be represented in a variety of ways, from fierce counterattack to passive resistance, and from panicked flight to silent withdrawal.

   ....

   ....

   ....

   ....

3. What is your personal "growing edge" where fear is concerned? Everybody is different. The important thing is to keep allowing God's love to transform you.

   ....

   ....

   ....

   ....

MEDITATION

Spend some time reading the rest of John's description of love and how it replaces fear and transforms relationships. Meditate on these verses in light of what you have just read:

Beloved, if God so loved us, we also ought to love one another. No one has seen God at any time. If we love one another, God abides in us, and His love has been perfected in us. By this we know that we abide in Him, and He in us, because He has given us of His Spirit. And we have seen and testify that the Father has sent the Son as Savior of the world. Whoever confesses that Jesus is the Son of God, God abides in him, and he in God. And we have known and believed the love that God has for us. God is love, and he who abides in love abides in God, and God in him. Love has been perfected among us in this: that we may have boldness in the day of judgment; because as He is, so are we in this world. There is no fear in love; but perfect love casts out fear, because fear involves torment. But he who fears has not been made perfect in love. We love Him because He first loved us. If someone says, "I love God," and hates his brother, he is a liar; for he who does not love his brother whom he has seen, how can he love God whom he has not seen? And this commandment we have from Him: that he who loves God must love his brother also (1 John 4:11-21).

Chapter 19

REVELATION BEYOND INFORMATION

Banning Liebscher

T HE APOSTLE PAUL PRAYED that we would *"know the love of Christ which passes knowledge..."* (Eph. 3:19). The verse concludes: *"that you may be filled with all the fullness of God."*

Experience is the key to fullness because it brings *revelation*. Without the revelation knowledge that comes by experience, we are limited to operating with only *information*. Most Christians have the correct information. In the majority of churches, if I were to ask, "Do you believe Jesus loves you?" I'm certain that 99 percent of the congregation would respond with a sincere *yes*. The mere fact that you are reading this book tells me that you probably believe Jesus loves you. But are you responding out of information or revelation?

When Evander Holyfield, the former heavyweight boxing champion, was in his prime, I loved to watch his fights. After seeing just a few of his fights, it became obvious to me that *he hits hard*. My observation was reinforced as I read the articles about his fights, listened to commentators talk about his boxing style, and heard other fighters being interviewed about their experiences with Holyfield in the ring. If you were to ask me, "Does Evander Holyfield punch hard?" I would say with conviction, "Yes. Evander Holyfield hits hard." But as strong and true an answer as that is, it is completely based in the realm of information. It doesn't actually become a *personal revelation* until I lace up the boxing shoes, slip on the boxing gloves, and step into the ring with Holyfield himself. About five seconds into the first round, when Holyfield's fist connects with my jaw and my knees buckle and little birdies begin to circle around my head, it's in *that* moment that revelation impacts me: "Evander Holyfield hits hard!" It's the exact same response as I would have given before, but now it's revelation—not purely information. I wouldn't only have read about how hard he punches; I would have experienced it for myself!

Too many people are content to live a life of information rather than revelation. But knowledge alone will never inflame a sustained blaze in you to love Jesus passionately. Only revelation will do that. Remember, Ephesians 3:19 says that the revelation that comes by experience is the key to fullness.

That Greek word translated "fullness" refers to a ship that is filled with merchandise and sailors. A ship can be seaworthy and underway toward a predetermined destination, but if you don't have the cargo on board or the manpower to sail the ship, you are not going anywhere. The same is true for us if we only have information without revelation and the reality of experience that brings God's fullness into our lives.

The revelation of His extravagant love will propel you deeper into God's heart because you will long to be with Him. The Civil War chaplain and champion of prayer, E.M. Bounds, wrote about those who have encountered the Father's love. He said, "They spend much time in prayer, not because they watch the shadow on the dial or the hands on the clock, but because it is to them so momentous and engaging a business that they can scarcely quit."[1]

Jesus said to His disciples: *"As the Father loved Me, I also have loved you; abide in My love"* (John 15:9). What a staggering statement. Jesus said that He loves us the same way God the Father loves Him. There isn't a greater love than that. He then called us to *abide* in that love. He didn't tell us to try to recreate the love we used to have when we first got saved and then abide in our love for Him, but to learn to abide in *His love for us*. He was saying, in essence, "My love for you is so extravagant. Your 'first works' are to learn to live a life connected to My exorbitant love." Every day we get the opportunity to abide in the most extreme, zealous, over-the-top, wild, mind-blowing love imaginable. As we learn to do that, our natural response will always be extravagant love for Him.

POINTS TO PONDER

1. Think of one or two pieces of information that you do not know by firsthand experience, similar to the Holyfield example. What would it take for that information to become experiential revelation?

    ....

    ....

    ....

    ....

2. Now think of one or two pieces of information about God that you do not know by firsthand experiential revelation. Would you like to know this information from a personal encounter with its Author? Put your desires into words as you tell Him.

    ....

    ....

    ....

    ....

3. What response do we have to an ongoing revelation of God's love? Do you know this as information or by revelation?

    ....

    ....

    ....

    ....

MEDITATION

First comes your experience of God's love, then comes your loving response. It is a cycle. Your pursuit of Him can really only ever be a response to His "courting." As Jesus declared, *"No one can come to Me unless the Father who sent Me draws him…"* (John 6:44). And you go out in search of God because He first initiated a revelation that He is pursuing you. Revelation 3:20 says, *"Behold, I stand at the door and knock…."* Jesus is the One standing at the door knocking. You didn't find Jesus; He found you. He wasn't lost; you were.

More importantly, God's quest to capture your heart did not stop when you became saved. He is still in pursuit of you, even today. Can you hear Him knocking on the door of your heart right now? What are you going to do?

ENDNOTE

1.   E.M. Bounds, *Power Through Prayer* (Springdale, PA: Whitaker House, 1982), 42.

Chapter 20

KNOWING GOD

Judy Franklin

BY DEFINITION, A RELATIONSHIP is a connection, behavior, or feelings toward somebody else—a friendship. That's the kind of relationship God wants with you. We can't know someone by just reading a book about him or her. To have a relationship we have to connect and interact with that person.

One day the Lord spoke to me. He simply said, "Ronald Reagan" (our president at the time). And that's all He said. I waited, but He said nothing else.

So I said, "Yes, he's our president."

Then God said, "You can read about him every day."

"Yes, I can read about him in magazines and books," I replied.

He said, "You can hear about him every day."

Well of course, I thought, *I could hear about him on the television, radio, or even in conversations with people who are discussing him or what he's doing.*

He went on, "And you are affected by what he does."

"Oh yes, he signs bills and laws that do affect my life."

Then He asked, "How well do you know him?"

Wow! I was brought up short. I didn't know Ronald Reagan at all. I really only knew *about* him.

The Lord said, "You can read about Me every day."

I responded, "Yes, in the Bible and different books."

He said, "You can hear about Me every day."

And I said, "Yes, on the television, radio, and at church."

Then the Lord said, "You are affected by what I do."

"Oh yes." I knew where this was going.

Finally, the Lord asked, "How well do you know Me?"

I realized then that I knew *about* Him, but I didn't really know Him on a personal basis. He wants us to know Him. His Son said,

> *No longer do I call you servants, for a servant does not know what his master is doing; but I have called you friends, for all things that I heard from My Father I have made known to you* (John 15:15).

The Lord has called us friends. It takes more than reading, hearing, or being affected by what someone does to actually be a friend. The heavenly realm is open to a new level of friendship. It is a mystery. How can we be friends with the God of the universe, the God of eternity, the God of power and might? Jesus said,

> *To you it has been given to know the mysteries of the kingdom of God, but to the rest it is given in parables, that "Seeing they may not see, and hearing they may not understand"* (Luke 8:10).

I don't want to be someone who just knows the parables. I want to know the mysteries. Don't you?

Out of this place of relationship come visions that connect our natural world to His spiritual realm. These visions release us not only into pure love, but also into a close connection with God.

These experiences with God will remove obstacles that keep us from receiving more of Him, learning more about Him, and becoming healed, whole, and intimate with Him. While you are experiencing His pure love, you discover you've stepped onto the path of your destiny.

I once read a quote attributed to Deitrich Bonhoeffer, a German theologian who was executed by the Nazis in World War II: "Truth divorced from experience must always dwell in the realm of doubt." Think about that. Truth without an experience can create a niggle of doubt in your mind. You may know God is able and willing to heal people, because the Scriptures say so, and you've read that Jesus healed everyone who came to Him. Yet you may struggle with thoughts that God is not willing to heal because you have never seen or experienced healing for yourself or someone you've prayed for.

It's important for you to have your own experiences with God. Our God is loving and kind and He wants an intimate relationship with us.

POINTS TO PONDER

1. If you think about your relationship with God as it compares with the level of your actual relationship with a human being (perhaps even some well-known person), how does it compare? Can you designate the name of a person with whom you engage at about the same level of interaction as you do with God? Do you wish you knew this person better? Along the same lines, do you wish you were closer to God?

    ....

    ....

    ....

    ....

2. Are you satisfied with the level of relationship you enjoy with God? What needs to change in order for it to improve? How can you reorient yourself so that your relationship can grow?

    ....

    ....

    ....

    ....

3. Do you know someone who is truly on a "first-name basis" with God? Are you one of those people yourself?

    ....

    ....

    ....

    ....

MEDITATION

Don't let yourself be disheartened when you realize how remote you are from God, even when you know you love Him. Instead, turn your face to His like a sunflower seeking the sun, basking in the warm rays and nodding its thanks. Ask God to take away one more brick in the wall between you and Him. Ask Him to show you how to cooperate with Him.

More than that, ask Him to show Himself to you in a new way, to melt your heart with His loving attention. He wants your friendship. He wants to relate to You more than you can ever want to relate to Him.

Chapter 21

POWER OF THE PRESENCE

Chris Overstreet

Living in the presence of God is living with our hearts' affection turned toward Heaven. When the presence of God rests on ordinary people, it changes the environment in which they live. We become a host for God and for His Kingdom, which is what enables us to demonstrate God's love and to manifest His Kingdom. Learning to host the presence is a major key to walking in the supernatural.

Our teams will often ask people if they have ever felt or experienced the presence of God. On one occasion, a young man was asked this in a park, and he said he had not. The team asked if he would like to, and he said yes. He was instructed to hold his hands out. As he did, a team member prayed that he would feel the person of the Holy Spirit. As he began to feel the presence of God on him, he described it as coolness or a tingling sensation running through his body. After he experienced God's presence, he was simply asked if he would like to receive Jesus into his heart. Without hesitation, he said yes. This is supernatural evangelism!

To live a life of miracles, signs, and wonders is not an option, but rather a heavenly mandate. As we host the presence of God, the raw power of God goes on display. Miracles, signs, and wonders point people to Jesus.

Paul wrote about himself and his fellow disciples:

> *For our gospel did not come to you in word only, but also in power, and in the Holy Spirit and in much assurance, as you know what kind of men we were among you for your sake* (1 Thessalonians 1:5).

Our lives are meant to demonstrate the same combination of word and power.

While picking up a friend of mine at the Sacramento airport, I walked by a group of women and told them that Jesus loved them. To my surprise, ten minutes later one of the young women from that group came over to me and asked if I could pray for her. I immediately said, "Yes, what can I pray for you about?"

She said, "My lover just left me, and my children have been taken from me." She explained to me that she was living a lesbian lifestyle. I told her that Jesus loved her and Jesus had a plan for her life. I told her that Jesus could transform her. As I was speaking those very words into her heart, the atmosphere around us began to change. She was probably expecting me to tell her that she was a sinner. But after I explained the love of the Father to her, her heart began to melt.

I asked her, "Would you like to receive Jesus into your heart and to be forgiven of your sins?" She said yes! So I led her in a prayer to receive Jesus Christ into her heart and to ask Jesus to forgive her of her sins.

After praying with her, I asked her if it was OK for me to lay my hand on her head and pray for her while in the airport. She said yes. I said, "Are you ready?" She said yes. I said, "Are you sure?" And she said yes. As I asked her the last time, I felt the power of God come upon me. I felt faith arise in my heart and the power of God that was at hand to see this woman's life completely transformed. As I laid my hand upon her head and began to pray, she fell out cold in the airport under the power of God!

While she was lying on the ground, people started to surround her and ask if she was all right. They said they were available to call 911. I told them, "No, that's OK! She's having an encounter with God right now." Two or three other people came by and asked if she was OK and also offered to call 911. One of them was a police officer.

The last gentleman who came over to her asked me what was going on and I told him she was having an encounter with God. He started to laugh in a mocking way. She sat up shortly after this gentleman began to mock her and said, "Let him laugh. He does not understand what just happened to me!"

I said, "What did you feel when I laid my hand on your head?" She said, "I felt fire go through me." She explained to me that she was planning on going home and committing suicide that night. But because of the encounter she had just had with God, her life now had hope.

When the saving power of God goes on display, it forces people to a decision. Jesus passed the baton of manifesting God's power and destroying the works of the devil to His disciples in the Great Commission. We are His disciples, and these signs will follow those who believe:

> *When He had called His twelve disciples to Him, He gave them power over unclean spirits, to cast them out, and to heal all kinds of sickness and all kinds of disease* (Matthew 10:1).

POINTS TO PONDER

1. When was the last time you experienced the power of God? Were you the "conduit" or did you receive what someone else handed on to you?

   ....

   ....

   ....

   ....

2. Have you ever been in a situation (perhaps your own conversion) when the power of God brought someone to salvation? Would you like to be in such situations in the future? What makes the idea attractive? What also makes it a little scary?

   ....

   ....

   ....

   ....

3. What does it mean to "host the presence of God"?

   ....

   ....

   ....

   ....

MEDITATION

Take time right now to be alone with God. Rest in His presence. As you relax your mind, turn your heart's affection toward His presence and allow Him to speak to you. Ask Him to show you how He sees you through His love. Draw on His presence to embolden yourself to bring supernatural encounters to others, as He leads.

You are a walking encounter with the powerful, living presence of God.

Chapter 22

A FRUIT-DRIVEN LIFE

Eric Johnson

W HEN YOU EAT AN apple, you are eating the fruit of an apple tree. A spiritual breakthrough or a victory is also called fruit. A fruit is not the same as a report, which is an account of the fact-grounded reality of a situation.

Often we will receive a reality report and a fruit at the same time. For example, for a number of years now at Bethel Church, we have seen tremendous breakthroughs for physical healing. One ailment that we have intentionally targeted is cancer. In fact, we have declared our city a "cancer-free zone."

Early on in this pursuit of a cancer-free city, we as a community of believers did not see as much breakthrough as we do now. We have had some great losses along the way, as well as great successes. But long ago, we made a decision to always keep our eyes on the fruit and not to let the reality of cancer determine what we do. In other words, we have kept our eyes on what God was doing instead of getting distracted by what was not happening.

Instead of looking at the reality of the strength of cancer ("giants in the land"), we have chosen to look at the fruit because the fruit is an invitation to own the land it came from. At the same time that we have been losing battles to cancer, other people have been getting healed of cancer. In this tension, we have refused to equally value the report and the fruit.

Choosing to cope with the problem rather than taking a stance directly against it weakens us. From experience, we have discovered that when we cope with something long enough, it begins to become our identity, and our ambition to defeat it dwindles. Then we forget about the problem. Immunity sets in; we become accustomed to it; it becomes normal.

Rarely does this happen overnight. It usually takes place over time. To keep it from happening, we need to take responsibility for stewarding the fruit as soon as it appears. From that day forward, we need to adjust our affections and attitudes.

By showing us the fruit, God intends to lure us into a Kingdom reality in which we can pick this fruit any time we want. We can always tell if we own the Promised Land when we can pick the fruit any time we want. When the nation of Israel saw the fruit, they had an opportunity to believe that God wanted them to live in the land it came from so they could have it any time they wanted. Instead, the Israelites decided to be distracted by the bad report.

In Israel's eyes, the report was bigger than the grapes that were brought back. They didn't realize that they had overlooked the fruit. Why did they overlook the fruit? For one thing, they expected that they were just going to walk into the land to occupy it. They didn't realize they'd have to fight and struggle. Little did the Israelites realize that they were required to win some victories to be able to occupy the land.

We're the same way. We get discouraged when our initial expectation of how things should happen doesn't materialize, so we slow down or completely stop in the direction we are going.

It doesn't have to be that way. I personally know a few individuals who own "promised land" in a spiritual sense. Some own financial land, and whatever they get involved with does really well financially. They have allowed the fruit of that land to lead them to a place of owning it. For others, it's authority over diseases; their success rate for healing certain diseases and illnesses is very high. They have allowed the fruit to lead them to a place of authority over these diseases and sicknesses.

Most of them didn't gain all this authority in a moment of time. For many it started with a small breakthrough, or maybe they heard a testimony of breakthrough. The fruit could have been as small as a grape or as big as a watermelon. No matter what size, it was still fruit. Often we have certain expectations of breakthrough, and when we don't see it happen to the level that we expected, we tend to overlook something that really is the key for greater breakthrough. We must learn to recognize fruit no matter how big or small.

So how do we begin to create a lifestyle that is fruit-driven and not reality-driven? First, we must develop an appetite for fruit. We must get hungry for that very thing. Hungry, we begin to aim our affection, actions, and attention to attaining more fruit. We make decisions and live our lives in constant pursuit of seeing the Kingdom invading the earth.

God intends for us to enjoy the fruit all the time. The Church has a tendency to believe that the fruit is for us to enjoy for a single moment; we don't realize it is bait that is meant to lure us to the Source.

POINTS TO PONDER

1. Name a "promised land" in your own life. How close are you to possessing it? What can you do to advance your pursuit? How have you chosen to focus your attention—on the breakthroughs and fruit or on the daunting realities of the situation?

    ....

    ....

    ....

    ....

2. Name one specific fruit in your own life, regardless of whether it's a grape or a watermelon in size. What have you done with this fruit? What can you do with this fruit now that you know about living a fruit-driven life?

    ....

    ....

    ....

    ....

MEDITATION

Psalm 68:19 states that He *"daily loads us with benefits."* God's desire is that we "eat fruit" all the time. Yet we often wonder why God can't just give us everything we need so we wouldn't need to fight for everything. But when we have to pay a price for something, we value it more highly. Then we not only have the ability to pick the fruit any time we want, but we also have the authority to administer it.

Start by recognizing the fruit that's showing up in your life right now. Decide that you're after the land that it came from and that you will not allow a bad report or giants to deter you from the course. Give God permission to set you on a journey through the land of giants so you can own the real estate all those fruit trees are sitting on.

Chapter 23

GLORY!

Paul Manwaring

I DOUBT THERE IS A greater word than *glory* except God Himself, for it holds together the entirety of the grand expression of His nature through time. As I have studied glory, I have learned more about the inherent unity and interrelatedness of all that God is and does. I expect that as the knowledge of the glory of God covers the earth, categories like "sacred/secular" and "natural/supernatural" will become less polarized in our thinking. Our lives will flow with the synergy that reflects and expresses the glory of God.

In the great plan of God, we are His glory carriers. Yes, Christ is the center of the plan, but in placing Christ at the center, God has placed us at the center, for He has placed us in Him and Him in us. As His Body, we corporately reflect His vast, unfathomable nature by individually contributing our own manifestation of His glory in every aspect of our lives and relationships. I often think of how His voice is like the sound of many waters and ponder that His ear must be able to hear every drop of water that flows over Niagara Falls. That ear, and the heart attached to it, can hear the cries of a victim and perpetrator of an offense at one and the same time. For us, such stretching of our thoughts and emotions at best challenges us and at worst causes us to polarize our views. But the more we study God's glory, the expression of His nature, the more we gain the capacity to allow its many facets to lead us ever deeper in comprehending and reflecting His magnificence, finally leading us into a life filled with wonder, joy, and worship—a life of glory.

Glory fills the pages of the Bible. But like many of the great, rich biblical words, glory often seems abstract and lacks an immediate connection in our minds and experience. And the images it does conjure up—crowns or heroic deeds—don't seem to help us much in comprehending the significance of what the Scriptures mean by the word.

"For the earth will be filled with the knowledge of the glory of the Lord, as the waters cover the sea" (Hab. 2:14). Interestingly, this verse is often misquoted by the simple omission of the word *knowledge*. This omission gives rise to a vision of the earth being gradually covered by a sort of vapor that drips down from Heaven and eventually engulfs the planet in bright gold. Wonderful though that vision might be, it can leave us waiting for an appearance of glory that is completely outside of us, distracting us from the powerful invitation in this verse—the invitation to *know* what glory is and ultimately to live in a world where everyone shares that knowledge.

Another reason we cannot afford to leave out knowledge from the promise of Habakkuk is that its omission turns the fullness of God's glory on the earth into a future event rather than a present reality. When the prophet Isaiah saw the Lord enthroned, he heard the angels declaring, *"The whole earth is full of His glory"* (Isa. 6:3). The truth is that God's glory is not far from us. It is actually the reality that surrounds us. The whole human history of falling short of the glory of God has not diminished it in any way. Neither has our failure to perceive it. It is impossible for us to erase God's glory from the universe. As C.S. Lewis wrote, "A man can no more diminish God's glory by refusing to worship him than a lunatic can put out the sun by scribbling the word 'darkness' on the walls of his cell."[1]

In light of Isaiah's vision that the earth is already full of God's glory, the prophecy of Habakkuk is God's promise that the gap between the immanent reality of His glory in the universe and our perception of that glory will be closed. The fullness of God's glory will be matched by the fullness of our knowledge.

In our world of the Internet and modern viral marketing, we are increasingly aware of how quickly experiences can multiply, and I like to think that these technologies are a parable of what this multiplication of knowledge may mean in part. Capturing an experience on a video or audio recording and sharing it with the world now takes hardly any time and effort at all. Through social networking Websites, one video clip can go overnight from one person to millions. One person can laugh at the antics of a little child, and with the sweep of a mouse, that experience can be transmitted to thousands of homes across the globe in seconds. The reproduction of information has become a part of our everyday lives.

Of course, how it will happen is secondary to that it will happen. We have been promised not merely that we will know about glory, but that we will experience it, live in it, and encounter it. And because God's glory is a present reality, it is a promise that we are invited to experience now.

POINTS TO PONDER

1. When you think of the word glory, what first comes to your mind? How did you learn this aspect of the meaning of the word?

....

....

....

....

2. Have you learned some of what you know about glory from reading about it? Have you learned some of what you know from the testimonies of others? Have you learned some from first-hand experience? How has your knowledge of the glory of God developed?

....

....

....

....

3. How have you experienced God's glory today?

....

....

....

....

MEDITATION

We were first created and then redeemed in order to be like God. No other part of God's creation was designated to bear His image; thus, no other part of His creation has the same glory we have. As Bill Johnson regularly points out, "Yes, God does say that He won't share His glory with another. But we're not another." We are made in His image—glorious! We are His Body, His Bride, and His children. We are not usurpers or pretenders; we are image-bearers. The knowledge of the glory of God in the face of Christ reveals our own glory—the glory He made us to share with Him from the beginning.

Keep praying for a greater depth and breadth of true knowledge of what this means.

ENDNOTE

1.   C.S. Lewis, *The Problem of Pain* (London: HarperCollins, 1964), 41.

Chapter 24

SUPERNATURALLY NATURAL

Judy Franklin

D O YOU UNDERSTAND WHAT can happen with your spirit in the spirit realm? You can actually internally see, hear, and speak with your spiritual eyes, ears, and voice.

I have found this concept often to be an obstacle to those who want to see into the spiritual realm, but who have difficulty doing so. First, we have to realize that it's not unlike seeing with our imaginations. Bob Jones, the prophet, uses the term "sanctified imagination." Pastor Bill Johnson says, "A sanctified imagination positions you for dreams and visions."

When you use your imagination, you form an image of something in your mind. You use your mind to see something that is not in front of your eyes at the moment. When you use your sanctified imagination, you aren't making anything up in your mind; what you are observing does not come from your mind. "Sanctified" visions and dreams come from the Holy Spirit. It's something that you experience.

Now, I can hear people say, "That's just vain imagination, and you'll go into error if you imagine stuff." I agree that there is a danger of error if we imagine things. But there is also a danger of missing out on incredibly powerful and godly experiences because of the fear of being deceived. There is also a danger in calling something unclean God has called clean.

I think my spirit has truly been made alive and my mind has been washed with the Word. Without claiming any sort of personal sinlessness or perfection concerning seeing in God's realm, I do think my sin nature has been crucified with Christ. It is not normal for me to sin (see Rom. 6). Sure, I can still do it (much to my chagrin), but it is no longer natural for me. So I have a great deal of trust in what Jesus did on the cross for us. With a renewed mind and heart and my spirit made alive and the Holy Spirit indwelling me forever, I have confidence that He can lead me.

Furthermore, Scriptures activate our imaginations all the time. The prophets and psalmists created plenty of images. For example, the only way I can "see" Zechariah's flying scroll (see Zech. 5:1-4) is by letting pictures move before my mind's eye. The Lord's prophets called Israel to imagine the judgment coming on them if they didn't return to the covenant and to imagine the blessings if they did. God was hoping this information and the mental pictures it created would move them to repentance. Imagination is just another access point for the Lord to reach us, as is language and music.

People wonder about who has the right to initiate these sorts of heavenly experiences—God or us. This concern usually arises when I help lead people to make themselves available for God to communicate with them in this way. It seems plain that God has the right to do so. And we all suppose that we are quite comfortable with this until someone begins to say he had a vision—then we get nervous! Can we ourselves initiate these sorts of experiences? I think we can at least ask and make ourselves available. My own experience is that sometimes heavenly experiences catch me by surprise, and at other times I am praying and waiting and hoping I get caught "by surprise."

Are these heavenly visions of the same type as people in the Bible experienced? Do they compare with Paul's experience of being caught up to the Third Heaven or with Ezekiel's visions? Well, they compare, but I don't claim that the things I am seeing and saying are on any level of the inspired, authoritative Scriptures. Truthfully, I have seen some things I don't understand and won't share until I do. I do not make a new doctrine or theology out of them. I just saw them.

In the Scriptures we can read about different sorts of supernatural experiences and visions. I and others have had a variety of heavenly experiences. During some of them it feels like I could "come out of it" whenever I want; other times I am lost in the experience. Always though, it feels like I am "going" somewhere, if that makes sense, and that I am being led, rather than leading, though I am free to ask questions and make requests. So it could be said that I am initiating some of the "action." In short, God and I partner in these times.

One day I talked to Bill Johnson about my concern about being deceived. He responded by saying, "Then your God is too small and your devil too big." I realized that I loved the Father, Jesus, and the Holy Spirit, and that the Holy Spirit was my guide and my teacher. I trust Him to lead me in righteous paths, and I stay accountable to the people He has given me. I know the Word.

So I'm no longer afraid of being deceived. Fear comes from the enemy, and he doesn't want us to experience God. And the truth is that Jesus knows my heart and is more than able to keep me in His ways. In his short epistle, Jude praised the God "*who is able to keep you from stumbling, and to present you faultless before the presence of His glory with exceeding joy*" (Jude 24).

POINTS TO PONDER

1. Do you feel that your spiritual senses are sharp enough to apprehend supernatural realities? Do you glimpse Heaven at times?

   ....

   ....

   ....

   ....

2. Can the devil draw believers into counterfeit experiences? How can you avoid deception? How can you tell when you are close to slipping into error?

   ....

   ....

   ....

   ....

3. What do you think would help you to experience more of God's heavenly realm? How can you position yourself to live a more "supernaturally natural" lifestyle?

   ....

   ....

   ....

   ....

MEDITATION

We need to exercise discernment and caution lest we be deceived by so-called spiritual experiences, but we cannot be so afraid of going into error that we "throw the baby out with the bathwater." We need to learn to eat the meat and spit out the bones. Ultimately, each of us is responsible for himself or herself, and it's important that we do not fear what other people think—and miss something that is meant for our good.

Ask your Lord and heavenly Father to guide you into all truth, including the truth about supernaturally natural experiences.

Chapter 25

ENCOUNTER

Beni Johnson

G OD HAS SO MUCH to teach us, and one of the ways He does this is through heavenly encounters with Him.

Judy Franklin and I were doing a women's conference in Georgia, and it was Judy's turn to teach in one of the sessions. She had told me she was going to share about her life and then lead everyone in having a heavenly encounter. I was so excited. I had not ever been in on hearing Judy lead people. I decided that I was not going to just sit and observe, but was going to jump right in and get all that I could get.

At the end of her sharing, she asked everyone who could to lie on the floor and get comfortable. Then she had us close our eyes and picture Jesus coming toward us. I immediately saw Jesus (my sanctified imagination is really alive and active). Judy then told us to see if He was saying anything to us. He told me that He loved me, and after that I don't remember what Judy said because I was caught up into Heaven.[1]

I looked down at my clothes and I was wearing a beautiful, full-length, white cotton dress. I looked up at Jesus, and He picked me up, turned around, and started walking toward a cottage. Before we got to the cottage, He put me down. I immediately knew that this was my cottage. The feeling that I was having during this time was joy. There was so much happiness. I was also feeling that this was the end of all time. All the generations were in Heaven. Eternity had started. As I was staring at this beautiful little English cottage with an English garden to my left and a grassy area to the right, I heard children coming around from the back of the cottage on the grassy lawn. The first child I saw was our oldest grandchild, Kennedy. When she saw me, she screamed to the other grandchildren, "Grandma is here now. We can play." And off she ran with the others.

All the time this was going on, I was crying, just bawling my eyes out, not out of sadness but out of sheer joy and happiness. I am a feeler, so feeling things is really important to me. Isn't it awesome that Father meets you right where it fits for you?

Anyway, I then turned to my right and looked in back of me and saw my fraternal grandmother, and she had many children with her. My dad's mom had been a Christian as long as I had known her. She had taught Sunday school for many years. She was an amazing woman. The day that my grandma retired from teaching Sunday school, she was called up on the platform at church, and the leaders were honoring her for all the years she had helped out. As she was standing there on the stage being honored by her church family, she collapsed from a stroke, and five days later, she went to be with Jesus.

When I saw her in Heaven with all those children, it thrilled me. I realized that what she was doing for God here on earth is what she was doing in Heaven. She loved the children, and she was now loving them in Heaven, too.

Then I looked again to my left side and saw my maternal grandmother. My mother's mom had been a pastor's wife for many years. But in those days she did not receive the honor that is given now to pastors and their wives. She became very bitter toward the church and my grandfather. She divorced my grandfather and lived for years in her bitterness, which eventually affected her physical body. But there were good times with Granny, and one thing I remember about her was her laugh. She was a big woman, and when she got tickled about something, she would throw her head back and open her mouth and laugh so loud you could see her tonsils. It made me so happy to see her happy. In this encounter when I saw her, she threw her head back and opened her mouth and let out a laugh that made me smile. God had erased all the hurts and she was Granny again.

I then turned my attention back to the cottage, and as I did, Bill's dad walked past me and stopped and looked at me. He said, "You are good for Bill." That's all he said, and it was enough.

During the entire encounter, I couldn't quite put my head around the feeling I was having. It felt familiar to me, but I couldn't figure it out. I just lay there on the floor resting in it, and then it hit me: this is peace. But what was different about this peace is that it was perfect peace. Perfect peace. Never had I felt so much peace before and so much perfection in it. It completely undid me. I didn't want to leave this feeling. There was no noise in my head. You know the kind I'm talking about— the kind that distracts you and makes you think too much. The war in my head was gone! I was lying in perfect peace. I did not want to leave. I felt that if I left this place, this peace would go away.

Then I remembered something my husband had recently taught. He had said that when God invites you into His vineyard and gives you a gift, it is always yours. You can have it whenever you want. That day I took the gift of peace, and I know that peace is my portion all the time. My head still gets in the way, but I'm working on that.

POINTS TO PONDER

1. What is the purpose of a heavenly encounter? Is it the same for everyone? Are all heavenly encounters like this one?

   ....

   ....

   ....

   ....

2. Have you ever felt that you were taken away by Jesus to experience a taste of Heaven? (Your experience does not have to be extensive.) If so, what was your "takeaway" from your experience?

   ....

   ....

   ....

   ....

MEDITATION

When we become open to having heavenly encounters, we need to be careful not to fall into pride or even necromancy (conjuring up the dead). It's better to just wait for God to split that wall between the visible and invisible so we can have a peek at the heavenly realm. He will do it when we least expect it.

Ask Him to keep you positioned at His feet so that, should He choose to bless you with such an experience, you will be ready.

ENDNOTE

1. Paul said, *"I know a man in Christ who fourteen years ago—whether in the body I do not know, or whether out of the body I do not know, God knows—such a one was caught up to the third heaven"* (2 Corinthians 12:2).

Chapter 26

READ TO HAVE A GOD ENCOUNTER

Bill Johnson

O UR YIELDED HEARTS ARE impressionable as we study the Bible and receive God's impressions (like fingerprints). Within that sort of tender soil, the Lord plants the seeds of His Kingdom perspective. The insights and empowering nature of the Scriptures provide solutions that are applicable to every society and culture. The Bible is limitless in scope, timeless, and complete, containing answers to every possible dilemma of humanity.

Our study of the Scriptures must take us beyond the historical settings, beyond language studies in the Hebrew and Greek, and at times beyond the context and intent of the human authors as to its content. Our reading of the Word must enable us to hear from God afresh. Repeatedly, His written Word must become the living Word in our experience.

I believe the Bible to be the Word of God, inerrant, fully inspired by the Holy Spirit. It is without equal, not to be added to or subtracted from. Not only did God inspire the writers, He inspired those who selected which respective writings should be included to make up the full 66 books of the Bible. I do not believe that there will be any new revelation that has the same authoritative weight as the Scriptures. It alone stands as judge of all other wisdom, be it the wisdom of people or an insight or book purported to be revealed directly from God or given by an angel. God is still speaking, but everything we hear must be consistent with what He has spoken to us in His Word.

In light of these burning convictions, the Church has instituted standards and traditions for our protection that practically suck the life and impact out of God's living Word. Although surely that was not the original intent, that has been an unintended result. The ability to hear God speaking to us, especially from His Word, is as necessary to our spiritual life as breathing is to our natural life.

Being unaware of His presence has cost us dearly, especially as we approach the Scriptures. King David, who wrote and sang songs about his love for God's Word, "set" the Lord before himself daily. He purposed to make himself regularly conscious of God's nearness, and he lived from that mindset.

The sanctified imagination is a tool in God's hand that enables us to tap into true reality. My approach is this: since I cannot imagine a place where He is not, I might as well imagine Him with me. This is not vain imagination. Rather it's vain to imagine otherwise.

One style of Scripture-reading is mainly concerned with finding and applying principles rather than enjoying His presence. This is good, but limited. Kingdom principles are real and powerful. They can be taught to anyone. When they are applied to life, they bring forth fruit for the King. Even unbelievers will experience blessing when they live by His principles. My friend was having financial problems. He confided in a neighbor, who happened to be a pastor, and the minister told him that his problems could be due to the fact that he wasn't honoring God with the tithe—10 percent of his income. He challenged my friend to test God by tithing to see if his counsel was accurate. When my friend tithed in response to the challenge, blessing started pouring into his life. He ended up giving his life to Christ because he saw and tasted God's love. But notice that the Kingdom principle functioned even before his conversion.

I am not knocking principles. The transformation of individuals, families, cities, and nations depends upon receptivity to Kingdom principles. However, this is not the core of a Christian's experience with the Bible. Rather, more often than not, we should read to have a God encounter.

The Word of God is living and active. It contains divine energy, always moving and accomplishing His purposes. It is the surgeon's knife that cuts in order to heal. It is a balm that brings comfort and healing. It is multidimensional and unfolding in nature. When Isaiah spoke a word, it applied to the people he spoke to, his contemporaries. Yet because God's Word is alive, much of what he said then has its ultimate fulfillment in another day and time. Living words do that.

POINTS TO PONDER

1. How and when have you found the Bible to be a closed book? In contrast, how and when have you found it to be life-giving? In retrospect, can you figure out what made the difference for you?

    ....

    ....

    ....

    ....

2. What parts of the Scriptures have you been reading lately? What has happened inside you as a result of your reading?

    ....

    ....

    ....

    ....

3. Today, what can you do to help cultivate your relationship with the third Person of the Trinity?

    ....

    ....

    ....

    ....

MEDITATION

It's difficult to get the same fruit as the early Church when we value a book they didn't have more than the Holy Spirit they did have. To value the Scriptures above the Holy Spirit is idolatry. It's not "Father, Son, and Holy Bible." The Bible reveals God, but is itself not God.

We must rely on the Holy Spirit to bring the words of the Bible alive. Without Him it is a closed book. Such dependency on the Spirit must be more than a token prayer asking for guidance before a Bible study. It is an ongoing relationship with the third Person of the Trinity that affects every aspect of life.

The Holy Spirit eagerly reveals His mysteries to all who are truly hungry. He makes us hungry in the first place and reminds us that our hunger cannot be satisfied except by receiving the love of God. Take your current level of hunger and ask Him to increase it even as He satisfies it. He will do it.

Chapter 27

LIFEGUARDS MUST BE SWIMMERS

Banning Liebscher

I ATTENDED VANGUARD UNIVERSITY IN Southern California. Vanguard is located in Costa Mesa, California, just a few minutes from some of the most spectacular beaches in America. Newport Beach and Huntington Beach became regular destinations for my friends and me, and it was there that I learned how to surf. I wasn't very accomplished at surfing, but I was able to surf shoulder-high waves and have a blast. I went into full-time ministry after college, and a few years later we took a youth group to Southern California for a retreat. I hadn't been surfing since I was in college, so a few of my friends and I decided we'd get up early one morning and surf for an hour or two.

When we arrived at the beach, the ocean looked a little crazy, but we decided to go out anyway. Big mistake! What we didn't know was that the largest swell to hit Huntington Beach in two decades was going to land that day. As you can probably guess, it didn't work out too well for me. I got caught in a set of waves in which I literally almost drowned. The current pulled me so strongly out to sea that I couldn't swim back in to shore, and I didn't have enough energy to get out past the waves that were coming in. So as wave after thunderous wave crashed in, I clung to my board for dear life and just tried to survive being repeatedly pushed under. The swells finally eased, and I was slowly able to swim to shore. It was an experience I will certainly never forget and one I don't care to attempt again.

In order to become a lifeguard, one must be an outstanding swimmer. It wouldn't make much sense if lifeguards did not know how to swim in the midst of waves. Can you imagine what might have happened if, while I was struggling to keep my head above water level, a well-intentioned guy had come out to save me—but then began to sink underwater himself? What if he didn't know how to swim that well and the wave scared him, too? If I'm ever drowning, I don't want someone like that to come and save me; I want David Hasselhoff, the famous television lifeguard, to rescue me and tow me ashore.

Many of us in the Church are as disadvantaged as the people we are hoping to save, because we don't know what God thinks about us or how He views us. Because we have not been secure in our identity, we have simply blended into the world. No wonder the drowning world around us has not come to us—because we look exactly like them.

Every day, all around us, people are experiencing a famine of love and power. They have never sensed the true love that comes from God. They feel unable to change; they are stuck in life. They live surrounded by sickness, depression, pain, and hopelessness. It is as if a storm is raging inside them, and they are powerless to calm it. They are searching for an answer, and that answer resides in you and me.

You have seen the bumper stickers that say, "Jesus is the answer." It doesn't matter what the question is; He is always the answer. Inside of you, you possess the answer to every question. When you got saved, Jesus and His Kingdom took up residence inside you. Power over death, sickness, hopelessness, sin, depression, and addictions now lives in you. You have experienced the first course of a banquet that is worth sharing.

Those who are in famine will always listen to those with food. The problem has been that we in the Body of Christ haven't looked as though we have any food. We've looked no different from the rest of the world.

Christians have been taught that the power of God is no longer available today, and they have protested against sinners rather than loving them.

It is time for us to have such an encounter with God that our identity changes. Then we will stop worrying about what the world thinks about us and be able to rescue the people around us who are floundering in the storm. We will be able to welcome them to the feast we are experiencing.

POINTS TO PONDER

1. "Christians have been taught that the power of God is no longer available today, and they have protested against sinners rather than loving them." Have you fallen into this trap yourself? Is it too late for a course correction where those particular sinners are concerned? In the context of the surfing example, what does it mean to hate the sin, but love the sinner?

   ....

   ....

   ....

   ....

2. Are you experiencing God's abundant feast? To switch the metaphor back again, have you learned to "swim"? If not, what can you do about it? If so, what can you do with your overflow of God's love?

   ....

   ....

   ....

   ....

MEDITATION

The world around you is drowning, and people you encounter in your daily activities are desperately seeking someone who knows how to swim. They are desperate for something they've never experienced—love and power. If they do not see love and power in you and your fellow Christians, then why should they listen to what you have to say?

Too many times, the Church makes Christians feel guilty for keeping the Good News to themselves. Instead, we need to create a culture that overflows with God's extravagant love and power. When we experience His abundant goodness, we find it natural to invite others to partake.

Today, rather than browbeating yourself for not reaching out to others, concentrate your prayers and actions on pursuing God's presence. Every day, begin the pursuit afresh. Ask Him for divine appointments so you can begin to give His goodness away.

Chapter 28

WE ARE PHYSICIAN'S ASSISTANTS

Kevin Dedmon

To say that we have the power to heal someone is inaccurate, but to say that we do not have the power to heal someone is equally inaccurate. We cannot heal anyone, but Christ in us can. We cannot set anyone free, but Christ in us can. We cannot save anyone from his or her sins, but Christ in us can.

Conversely, it is almost as if God will not heal, deliver, and save without us. Certainly God has the power to heal us on His own. But God, in His sovereignty, has chosen to partner with believers to bring His Kingdom rule to the earth, just as He did when He commissioned Adam in Genesis 1:28 to *"fill the earth and subdue it."* Obviously God had the power to rule the earth, but He chose to give the responsibility and authority to us.

In Matthew 10:8, Jesus told His disciples to give away what they had freely received. What had they freely received? "[Jesus] *gave them power over unclean spirits, to cast them out, and to heal all kinds of sickness and all kinds of disease"* (Matt. 10:1). In Matthew 28:18, Jesus said, *"All authority has been given to Me in heaven and on earth,"* implying that He was giving His authority to the disciples so that they could represent and expand His Kingdom. Therefore, with authority comes inherent responsibility.

Many wonder why more people are not coming into the Kingdom. After all, we have the truth—the Good News! Maybe it is because we are waiting for others who are "gifted" to do what we have all been given responsibility and authority to do. If we could grasp the ramifications of the fact that we have already been commissioned and authorized to go represent the Kingdom, maybe we would have more confidence to release what is already inside of us. His Kingdom would come.

Here is an example. A pastor took my son, Chad, and me to a hospital to pray for a woman who was very ill. On the way to her room, I noticed the emergency room waiting area filled with people needing attention.

On the way out after praying for the woman, I asked the pastor to wait while we took a detour into the emergency room waiting area. I announced the good news: "If anyone does not want to wait for the doctor, I can take care of you now."

You see, wherever I go, I think of myself as a Physician's assistant. I assist the Great Physician in bringing the Kingdom wherever I find a need that demands the coming of the Kingdom.

Oddly enough, however, when I asked if anyone needed healing, they all just shook their heads. "Well, that's strange," I replied, "because I felt like God wanted to heal someone's knee."

Still, they shook their heads in denial until the son of an elderly man piped up and said, "Wait a minute, Dad, your knee is so messed up that you have to wear a brace and can barely walk!" The man reluctantly pulled up his pant leg, revealing a brace that extended from the middle of his thigh to the middle of his calf.

I asked if he would like me to take care of his knee, but to my surprise, he shook his head and said, "Oh, no thanks, I'm OK," to which I responded, "How can you be all right when you can barely walk?" Without hesitation, I began to wave my hand toward him as I said, "God, release Your goodness on this man. Just be healed in Jesus' name."

Immediately, the man invited me to come closer (he was apparently sensing God's presence) and then enthusiastically asked me to place my hand on his knee. After I prayed for a short time, he showed signs of improvement. He started moving his leg around and flexing his knee with a look of astonishment.

Meanwhile, his daughter began motioning to her neck and shoulder and asked if I could also help her. She had been in a car accident and had been in pain ever since. With the elderly father now healed, I moved over to release God's healing presence on his daughter. In less than two minutes, all of the pain left and she had complete mobility.

During this time, Chad also spoke out a word of knowledge for someone with back pain, which turned out to be for another family member of the elderly man. After Chad prayed for a few minutes, the man started bending down at the waist, proving he had been completely healed.

As I walked toward the exit, I had to walk past the man whose knee had just been healed. As I started to pass by, he reached out, grabbed my hand, and pulled it down to touch his other knee, which also needed healing. As my hand touched his knee, he was instantly healed!

POINTS TO PONDER

1. Rhetorical question: What would happen if all of us waited for someone more gifted to perform the works of the Kingdom? Where would these "more gifted" people come from? Where should you look for them?

   ....

   ....

   ....

   ....

2. Was it convenient for Kevin and Chad to stop in the ER waiting room? What if they had waited for those people to come to them for the sake of convenience as well as absolute certainty that they wanted to be prayed with for healing? Why did they do what they did?

   ....

   ....

   ....

   ....

3. Have you ever considered yourself the Physician's assistant? What was the result?

   ....

   ....

   ....

   ....

MEDITATION

After Peter and John healed the cripple at the Beautiful Gate, the onlookers were amazed at what they had just witnessed. There seemed to be an underlying sentiment that Peter and John were some kind of super-heroes with special power that made them unique. Peter, most likely recognizing this attitude, responded:

> *Men of Israel, why do you marvel at this? Or why look so intently at us, as though by our own power or godliness we had made this man walk?* (Acts 3:12)

Then, after a short sermon, he added:

> *His name, through faith in His name, has made this man strong, whom you see and know. Yes, the faith which comes through Him has given him this perfect soundness in the presence of you all* (Acts 3:16).

Sadly, many people shy away from the supernatural gifts, thinking that they do not have the power to perform supernatural feats. The reality is that they don't. None of us have the power to heal, save, prophesy, or set people free; nevertheless, God has commissioned us to go and do these things—to make the world a better place to live. What else can we do but obey?

Chapter 29

DOES THE KINGDOM
NEED REVIVAL?

Eric Johnson

REVIVAL HAPPENS WHEN SOMETHING that once was dead becomes infused with life. For many, the word revival is synonymous with church meetings in which the power of God shows up and people surrender themselves to Jesus and get healed of various sicknesses. We make a hobby of reading the old revival stories, and we can't help but get excited. We begin to set our hearts toward it happening again.

Let me pose a couple of questions. Does the Kingdom need revival? Did Jesus need revival? If the Kingdom is meant to create life and continues to create life, then is revival necessary? I am suggesting that it is possible for us never to need personal revival because we never lost life in the first place. Even so, there will be times and seasons when this infusion of life is heightened, but in general there is a steady flow of life. As the Body of Christ, we need to carry the mindset that whatever God creates is also meant to continue to create life.

The word *revival* actually means "restoration of life." It's a word we typically use for a move of God of some capacity. As we study the history of revival, we find evidence of a certain repetition. Wherever moves of

God take place, people's lives are transformed, cities and nations are changed, and people are touched by God. Miracles and healings take place, marriages are restored, and businesses prosper. Then the revival seems to die out as the generation that it started with begins to pass away.

You can look into history and see moves of God that ended because of people's decisions. Revivals fade because people stop co-laboring with God. When we co-labor with Him, things begin to multiply and generate momentum. When we stop co-laboring with Him, we are usually at the beginning of the end.

The Law was designed to show people what was required of them outside of relationship with God. When we can't live in relationship, then the Law is a default to show us how to live our lives. But it is always impossible to uphold the Law. Then instead of moving away from the Law and moving into relationship with God, people decide to work even harder at keeping the Law, which leads them to be enslaved by something lifeless.

The Law becomes entrenched in a lifestyle of slavery to a list of words, and it gives people no hope of freedom. It wreaks havoc on people's ability to see God as loving. The paradigm ends up becoming bent; God is viewed as an angry God. Fear becomes the lens and filter through which people lived their lives. People become powerless, which further reduces their ability to make moral decisions that bring life. It also reduces their ability to live in relationship.

In the Kingdom of God, life continues to create life. Genesis tells the detailed account of how God created the world that we live in. When God spoke, His words created life. Not only that, they set in motion something that hasn't stopped. Creation as we know it has been reproducing, adjusting, and expanding since it was first spoken into existence. During Creation, He said, *"Let there be light"* (Gen. 1:3), and it's still working! This truth intrigues me immensely. It is evident that God is in the business of *sustaining* life. This life manifests the Kingdom of God throughout the earth.

In the Old Testament, when God blesses a nation, many times you will see other nations come and ask, "What must I do to get what you have?" It's God's ultimate marketing strategy: people become jealous for who He is.

In Psalm 67:1-2, we read, *"God be merciful to us and bless us, and cause His face to shine upon us, that Your way may be known on earth, your salvation among all nations."* The writer knew that when God's favor is upon the people, the supernatural will naturally happen, and His Kingdom will be established on earth: *"Then the earth shall yield her increase; God, our own God, shall bless us"* (Ps. 67:6).

I can't help but think what it will be like when we believers step into this reality of God's face shining upon us; one of the results will be the earth responding by "yielding her increase." What happens in the spiritual will be manifested in the natural.

POINTS TO PONDER

1. How have you thought about "revival"? Have you assumed that it would fade out over time? Why or why not?

   ....

   ....

   ....

   ....

2. Have you experienced true revival in your life as a believer? What were its primary features? With whom did you experience it? Are you still experiencing that same revival today? Do you know why?

   ....

   ....

   ....

   ....

3. Do you know firsthand what it means to labor in your own strength to sustain a move of God? Do you know firsthand what it's like to co-labor with God to achieve the same result? With this in mind, evaluate a slice of your own history as a believer.

   ....

   ....

   ....

   ....

MEDITATION

We need to understand the supernaturally natural momentum of God's Kingdom. We also need to learn about our role in sustaining this momentum. The Church as a whole has largely missed this principle. We know how to enjoy life as it happens to us, but we don't seem to know how to steward life into a place of increase and inheritance.

Offer yourself to God as a co-laborer in His Kingdom harvest fields. Ask Him to keep you reliant on His Spirit for all you do and to protect you from "building a booth" (see Luke 9:28-33) to capture and preserve His ever-living presence. Tell Him that you want to remain attentive and obedient to Him and that you do not want to fall back on a rule-bound, default way of living.

Chapter 30

SHEKINAH GLORY

Paul Manwaring

*S*HEKINAH GLORY. THROUGHOUT MY Christian life, I have often heard this phrase and assumed I basically understood it. *Shekinah* often comes up when people are describing the most striking supernatural appearances of the glory of God. The very sound of the word seems to evoke a sense of mystery and awe. I always assumed it was a biblical word, but when I began to study *Shekinah,* I was surprised to learn that this word is never actually used in the Scriptures—and that it has a more specific meaning than I had thought. (This is true of many of the words we use to express biblical ideas. You'll never find the words *Trinity* and *incarnation* in the Scriptures, either, though these concepts are directly derived from what is written there.) *Shekinah* is one of the oldest of such theological terms.

Shekinah means "the dwelling place of Him who dwells." Thus, my study Bible notes *Shekinah glory* in the margins whenever the words *glory* (the manifest presence of God) and *dwelling* or *abiding* appear together.

God is the God who dwells. This is one of the primary dimensions of His glory, and unless we establish this in our thinking, we will not be prepared to see that glory. It is possible to gain the impression that, rather than being the God who dwells, God is more of a visitor to the world He created. In the Old Testament, vast stretches of time are unaccounted for; it seems as though manifestations of the presence of God were few and far between. But when we trace *Shekinah* more closely through the Scripture, looking for the God who dwells, we discover a beautiful progressive revelation of God's eternal plan to dwell with us.

In the beginning, God and people dwelt together. We can't imagine what that "household" must have been like; all we really know is that when Adam and Eve sinned, they had to leave it. Consequent to the Fall, the human race became homeless, barred from our original dwelling in God's glory by cherubim and a flaming sword.

Centuries later, on top of a mountain engulfed in a supernatural cloud, Moses saw those cherubim again when God instructed him to build a replica of His heavenly dwelling. God wanted an outpost among His exiled people, one that would begin to reveal His desire to bring them back to their true home. As a result, all of Israel knew where the Shekinah was, for they witnessed two of its primary manifestations, the cloud and the fire. From then on, the cloud and the fire of the Shekinah became the center of Israel, their true home. Whenever it moved, they moved. (See Exodus 40:36-38.)

Centuries later, David's desire to build a house for the Lord was the most obvious expression of the "one thing" he desired—to dwell with the Lord (see Ps. 27:4). It so happened that dwelling with His people was also the thing in God's heart. Moreover, what was in God's heart was this mutual desire of people and God to dwell together. This is why God didn't choose a city or a building, but rather a man after His heart, and then fulfilled what was in the man's heart. Though He wouldn't let David build the temple, He gave him the detailed plans for it, just as He had done for Moses (see 1 Chron. 28:19), enabling Solomon to build it. After the massive seven-year project was completed, He moved into it.

Fittingly, the arrival of the Shekinah in this new home was accompanied by something that hadn't been present at the tabernacle of Moses. At the temple, the cloud descended amidst a glorious concert of His people making "one sound," because this house was a manifestation of the mutual desire of God and people to dwell together. After the cloud, the fire came once again, in the sight of the whole nation. (See Second Chronicles 7:1-3.)

The Shekinah remained in Solomon's temple for just over 400 years while tragically, the people of Israel failed to remain faithful to their covenant with God, resulting in their captivity in Assyria and Babylon. In a dramatic vision he received early in this captivity, the prophet Ezekiel witnessed the departure of the Shekinah from the temple as the Lord brought judgment on the city. (See Ezekiel 8–10.)

The biblical accounts of the rebuilding of the second temple do not record the return of the Shekinah. The sShekinah did not return to that building because once again, God had chosen a man instead. This man was called both the Son of David and the Son of God. Jesus announced that He was the next revelation of Shekinah, the dwelling of Him who dwells (see John 14:10-11,20).

Jesus came, not just to tabernacle among us, but to make us part of that tabernacle. The great mystery of the cross is that, by allowing the house of His body to be destroyed, Christ was positioned to rebuild it, and in rebuilding it, to bring all of humanity into the house, to make us His Body. From this point on in the Scriptures, the "temple" or "house" of God is always connected to the Body and bodies of believers.

An ancient father of the Church, John Chrysostom, wrote, "The true Shekinah is Man." We must not hold back from stepping into the fullness of what we are called to as carriers of the Shekinah glory.

POINTS TO PONDER

1. Within the Church, Shekinah glory has sometimes been applied as a descriptive term for loud, expressive, worship-filled experiences. Historically, was it always manifested this way? In what variety of ways has it been displayed?

   ....

   ....

   ....

   ....

2. How does the Shekinah glory show forth in the Body of Christ?

   ....

   ....

   ....

   ....

3. How do you participate in manifesting God's Shekinah glory to the world?

   ....

   ....

   ....

   ....

MEDITATION

Shekinah describes the glory of "the God who dwells," and *dwelling* is one of the primary characteristics of His glory. Unless you understand this, you will not be prepared to see that glory. Solomon's priests and people witnessed the moment that God took up residence in the temple in all His glory:

> *The glory of the Lord filled the temple. And the priests could not enter the house of the Lord, because the glory of the Lord had filled the Lord's house. When all the children of Israel saw how the fire came down, and the glory of the Lord on the temple, they bowed their faces to the ground on the pavement, and worshiped and praised the Lord...* (2 Chronicles 7:1-3).

Allow your own heart to become a more welcoming dwelling place for God's Spirit. Pray that you and the members of Christ's Body with whom you share your life will become and remain pure vessels for His glory.

Chapter 31

POST-KATRINA MIRACLES

Chad Dedmon

W HEN I AM WITH my friends, I see greater outbreaks of the Spirit than when I am alone. It's a Kingdom principle that unity in the Spirit releases a greater anointing for breakthrough.

For example, after Hurricane Katrina in 2005, I went with a group of my friends to the Houston Astrodome to minister to the disaster victims. Years earlier, we had dreamed about the day when we would be in stadiums together praying for multitudes. When the opportunity came, we knew we had to "strike while the iron was hot." So even though we all had full-time jobs, we decided to drop what we were doing and go to Houston.

The stadium was on lockdown for health and safety reasons, and we had been told that you had to be a certified Red Cross worker or part of a media team in order to enter. We walked up to the front gate and sure enough, the National Guard security officer barred us. Feeling somewhat deflated, we started walking back to our car, when I suddenly remembered a prophetic word I had received before leaving home.

Friends had told me that when we arrived at the Astrodome, the door would be closed, but the next door to the left would be open. I had interpreted this to mean a spiritual door, but suddenly I realized that it was a literal door. I told the team, "Let's try the next door on the left." We walked up to the security guards there, and they ushered us right through, no questions asked.

After the miracle of getting inside, our excitement grew exponentially as we prayed to see what God wanted to do. Right away, we met a lady with three herniated disks who was bedridden in her cot. She let us lay hands on her back and pray. She said she was feeling electricity in her back. We asked her to check it out, and to our amazement, she got right up and started touching her toes, with full range of motion. Overjoyed, she screamed, "Look at this, I couldn't do this before!" She became our evangelist as she shouted to everyone in the vicinity, "Look at this, I am healed; you need to have these people pray for you."

She brought over a man in a wheelchair, trying to convince him that if we prayed for him, he would be healed. While we were praying for him, my friend Chris Overstreet saw a lady with a wrist brace walking by and he told her, "Excuse me, ma'am, God is healing your wrist right now." She took off her wrist brace and realized that she had no pain.

People began gathering to receive prayer. Other people were passing by and watching this crazy scene. A portal of God's presence continued to intensify. One lady walked by, and as she entered the area, she was instantly slain in the Spirit without anyone touching her. Unknowingly, the lady had walked right through the center of this portal and got touched by the Holy Spirit. A police officer rushed up to find out what happened. Calmly, Chris told him, "It's OK, officer, God is touching her."

After a few minutes, the lady came to and started confessing that she was an alcoholic. She explained that she had not had anything to drink in the past few days, so she was experiencing alcohol withdrawal sickness as a result. She told us, "Whatever it was that just touched me is the answer for my life." We started praying for the spirit of addiction to leave and for her to be filled with the Spirit. She began laughing uncontrollably and rolling around on the floor exclaiming, "It feels so good!"

Then we discovered that the first lady, whose back had been healed, was a grandmother. Her daughter and granddaughter were watching everything. I started talking to the daughter and had an open vision of her as a five-year-old girl. I explained that the Father wanted to heal something that had happened to her when she was five. With tears streaming down her face, she began to receive the Father's love. I asked, "Do you want to know Jesus as your personal Lord and Savior?" She responded, "Yes, as long as you pray for my daughter (who happened to be five years old) to know Jesus, too." As they started praying to receive Jesus, the grandmother said, "I want to know this Jesus, too; don't leave me out!" So the whole family prayed together to receive Jesus.

Chris and I found a lady whose spine had been severed in a car accident two years earlier, who was living in a wheelchair, no longer able to walk. As Chris and I prayed for her, the power of God started flowing into her spine.

Right then, a man screamed out at me, "What did you just do to me? You did some kind of voodoo thing to me." A little taken aback, I replied, "What happened to you?" He explained that as he was walking by, he felt a surge of energy go through his knees and that furthermore he had had two failed operations on his knees. So I told him, "Move your knees and check them out." He began jumping in the air and doing leg squats, testing out his knees, and started laughing as he said, "I feel like I have new knees; there is no more pain or restriction!"

I explained to him, "What you just experienced isn't voodoo; Jesus healed you because He loves you." We turned our attention back to the lady in the wheelchair and asked her to check out her spine. On her own initiative, she got up out of her wheelchair and walked hundreds of feet for the first time in two years.

We spent several days in the Astrodome, and we saw many more outbreaks of the Spirit. These were only some of the stories. My friends and I had to pinch ourselves as we realized that our dreams were becoming a reality right before our eyes.

POINTS TO PONDER

1. Do you have a vision for partnering with friends in various ministry settings? In your experience, how has teamwork made a difference?

    ....

    ....

    ....

    ....

2. As they endeavored to follow the Holy Spirit, what kinds of risks did these friends take? What were the personal costs of doing ministry together? How did they support each other? Would you say that they were closer friends after they left the Astrodome?

    ....

    ....

    ....

    ....

3. What is the ultimate purpose of team ministry?

    ....

    ....

    ....

    ....

MEDITATION

If your excitement level has risen while reading this account (or if you have found yourself thinking of another kind of Spirit-led ministry in which you wish to participate), ask God to help you find relationships that will cause you to step into your supernatural destiny. Ask Him to release favor and grace for you to discover your spiritual fathers and mothers, brothers and sisters. Tell Him you want to knit together your heart and dreams with trusted, godly friends. A Jonathan and David kind of friendship is not too much to ask for.

Chapter 32

SIGNS THAT MAKE YOU WONDER

Bill Johnson

SOMETIMES WE SEE HIGHLY unusual situations, such as Moses' burning bush, that seem to have no meaning in and of themselves. God brings those events into our lives to get our attention, hoping we will "turn aside" from our agendas and plans. *"When the Lord saw that he turned aside to look, God called to him from the midst of the bush and said, 'Moses, Moses!' And he said, 'Here I am'"* (Exod. 3:4).

We have a pre-service prayer meeting in the church dining room on Friday nights. One night I got there a bit early to pray alone. Soon after my arrival, a roadrunner with a lizard in its mouth came up to the wall of windows facing the west. He started to dance and jump at the window as though he was trying to get inside. I have spent quite a bit of time outdoors. I had never seen a roadrunner in my life and never even heard of one in northern California. I got within three feet of him and thought, *This is too strange to not be prophetic.*

Minutes later, he left. Others came to pray, and the room began to fill up. Then the roadrunner returned. One of my staff members said, "Oh, the roadrunner's back." I asked what he meant. He said, "Yeah. He was here last week."

For the next several months, the roadrunner came to most every prayer meeting, usually with a lizard in its mouth. Some of our youth leaders began to meet in the dining room to pray before their main meeting on Wednesday nights. The roadrunner started to come to that prayer meeting as well, usually with a lizard in its mouth. I used to have a Signs and Wonders class on Sunday mornings. One morning I talked about the "signs that make you wonder" and used the roadrunner as an illustration. Almost on cue, he came up to the window as before. The people pointed and said, "You mean him!" I was shocked because he came almost on cue.

News began to spread about this strange, recurring event. Many tried to help by doing research to find the meaning. I was told that the roadrunner is related to the eagle. They're one of the few creatures that will kill and eat a rattlesnake, which we do have in our area. I already knew that eagles represent the prophetic and snakes usually speak of the devil. It brought great joy to know that the enemy would be trampled down through the increase of the prophetic.

During this time we started building our 24-hour prayer chapel called The Alabaster House. The roadrunner started to shift his focus from our prayer meetings to that building. He would actually perch himself on a rock that many of our folks had taken to calling the Eagle Rock because of its unusual resemblance to the head of an eagle. It was as though the roadrunner, who loved prayer meetings, was overseeing the prayer-house building project.

One day he got inside the church facility, right above the original prayer room. One of our custodians, Jason (an extremely prophetic student in our school of ministry), found the bird in a large second story meeting room. Jason turned on some worship music and sat in the middle of the room on the floor and worshiped the Lord. The roadrunner came over right in front of him and seemed to join him. He would occasionally leave Jason and go to the window as though he wanted to go outside, but then he would come back and stand right in front of Jason as he worshiped.

Jason started to feel bad for taking so much time for worship while he was supposed to be cleaning, so he turned the music off and went downstairs to clean other rooms. The roadrunner went with him. Suddenly someone opened the door in the long hallway and startled the bird. He flew to the end of the hall, hit the plate glass window, and died instantly.

This bird had become like a beloved mascot to us. He had come during a time when the finances were extremely tight. The lizard in his mouth spoke to us of God bringing all that was needed for this move of God. As eagles represent the prophets, it was obvious that the prophetic was actually getting stronger and stronger within our church body.

Jason found me to tell me this horrible news. I asked him to show me where he had put the bird so we could go and raise it from the dead. With a sense of purpose and confidence, we walked to where the bird was lying. It made perfect sense to me that God would want the roadrunner alive. Why should He want our living prophetic message dead? Strangely, though, I felt the anointing lift when I got about five or six feet away from the bird. It puzzled me. God's presence had been upon me in a strong way until I got close. It was as if He was saying my resolve was good, but my application and timing were not.

The roadrunner was not raised from the dead. We were quite sad. Then the Lord spoke, "What I am bringing into the house has to have a way of being released from the house, or it will die in the house."

That word applied to the money we desperately needed, the manifest gifts of the Spirit we were crying out for, the specific anointings we were growing in, and the people who were being saved. The word was costly and clear: *we only get to keep what we give away.*

POINTS TO PONDER

1. Although this unusual prophetic sign occurred in the past and in a particular church, where it carried a specific meaning, what did you learn from reading about it? Add that new information to other things you have learned about hearing God's voice.

   ....

   ....

   ....

   ....

2. Does God send prophetic signs only to people who serve in a leadership or spokesperson capacity, such as Moses or Elijah? How do you know?

   ....

   ....

   ....

   ....

3. Do unusual events always point to something prophetic? Why or why not? How can you know?

   ....

   ....

   ....

   ....

MEDITATION

God sometimes speaks to us by hiding truths in phrases, stories, riddles, and circumstances. The meaning is there for us to find. When we lean into God, anticipating His voice, it becomes easier to discern when those circumstances are from God or are merely unusual events in life. God's unique language of hidden meanings becomes an invitation to enter His great adventure.

Take time to "lean into" God right now, especially if you have been puzzled by something that seems to be a prophetic sign. If He doesn't explain it to you today, keep listening and pondering until you have an answer.

Chapter 33

REVIVAL MESSINESS

Danny Silk

I FOUND THAT I HAD a secret expectation that revival would eliminate all the problems in my environment. I realized it when one day I felt a wave of unbelief because of the people's problems surrounding me—adultery, child abuse, addictions, lying, and more. I thought to myself, *If God is really here and His Kingdom is coming, then why are so many people still messing up their lives?* That question caused me to think about the Kingdom of God as I never had before. Is Heaven a place where God controls all the choices? What about the Garden? That place had choices.

I realized then that Heaven has poor choices in it. This must be the case, because it's a free place. Lucifer found a poor choice. I have since heard Bill Johnson say many times, "Grace in a culture gives the sin that resides in people's hearts an opportunity to manifest." When we live in a place of revival love and acceptance and are applying God's unconditional love to people's lives 100 percent of the time, the sin that lies dormant in people's lives, or the sin that people have been struggling with or hiding, will come out and end up on the floor.

Therefore, we had better have a mechanism in our Christian culture that deals effectively with the sin when it comes out. For whatever reason, we've come to expect that church is a place where there isn't going to be any sin. It's just not true. If we don't know how to deal with sin, then we don't know how to deal with people. We inevitably create a culture of law in order to keep people from sinning. The message of this culture is, "Contain your sin within yourself. Don't show it to me. I can't handle it."

Remember, this was the Pharisee's line. They were famous for being afraid of sin, largely due to the fact that their only remedy for sin was punishment. The fear of punishment ruled their hearts, relationships, and culture. Jesus, on the other hand, had a group of unlikely companions. They were thieves, tax collectors, and hookers. Compared to the other religious leaders at the time, He was like "Jesus of Vegas."

Jesus was not the least afraid of the messes people made. Even the people who spent three years walking with Jesus personally were still making messes the night before His Crucifixion. But ultimately, His love and the way He led people empowered them to rise above their mistakes and issues.

Without Spirit-aided self-control, we live in constant reaction to one another, which creates a culture of power struggle and blame. "Your stuff triggers my stuff, and I don't know what to do when you do that. Stop it! Now I am going to blame you for what I do...."

Messes create a toxic environment for everyone, so we must confront the messes head-on—but in love and honor. The purpose of loving confrontation is to bring something to the light. When I go to a person in a spirit of gentleness, I go to turn the lights on for that person. I want the person to see. I do not need to control that person's response. My goal is to help the person see the mess he or she has made and to find in me a helpful ally in overcoming it. Kingdom confrontation is a process of empowerment, not domination. We steal people's option for freedom when we try to control the outcome, because we disempower them and create irresponsible victims.

In a culture of rules, not only do people expect punishment when they fail, but they are overwhelmed with shame. Shame isn't just a feeling; it is a *spirit* that attacks the identity of the individual. This spirit lies to the person, saying, "You didn't just fail; you are a failure. You didn't make a mistake; you *are* a mistake."

It's easy for us to forget our true identities after we have failed. But when someone reaches in and confronts us with our true identities, it is an act of love that will live on far longer than the sting of failure and consequences. We can rise above our fear and shame. We can regain our clear thinking and our relationships with others and with God.

Confrontation is a process of applying pressure to another person's life, on purpose, to expose the broken spots. We can't make better decisions and create a different result until we know what is wrong. Isaiah 1:18 says:

> *"Come now, and let us reason together,"* says the Lord, *"Though your sins are like scarlet, they shall be as white as snow; though they are red like crimson, they shall be as wool."*

In other words, though your sins are blatantly all over the place, God says, "We can do something about that." There is hope. More importantly, God says, "Come, let us reason together." The very heartbeat, nature, and desire of God are that we *come*. He invites us to look at something mutually to correct it.

POINTS TO PONDER

1. Have you, too, carried a subconscious assumption that revival would solve every problem and make life trouble-free? As you have been disappointed repeatedly, how have you come to understand what a revived Kingdom culture looks like? Have you despaired of finding a way out of the repeated difficulties? Why or why not?

    ....

    ....

    ....

    ....

2. Do you enjoy a healthy church environment? Do you think yours represents a culture of grace? How can you tell?

    ....

    ....

    ....

    ....

3. Consider a real-life relationship situation in which you or another person within your church sinned. Prayerfully, in your mind, revise the details of the event with elements of grace that you have learned about since then.

    ....

    ....

    ....

    ....

MEDITATION

God invites each one of us to come and reason with Him, to see what He sees and to hear what He has to say about it. Yet on our own, particularly when our sins have overwhelmed our emotions, we find it nearly impossible to approach Him. That's why we need each other. We need to usher each other into the light of His presence so that we can see our broken places and hear His voice so that we know what to do about them.

Approach Him now and ask Him not only for light, but for friends who will walk with you as together you live out a culture of grace and revival.

Chapter 34

FOUNTAIN OR CISTERN?

Judy Franklin

W E HAVE A TENDENCY to try to control what God is doing. God gave me a lesson on this subject one day after I read the following Scripture:

> *For My people have committed two evils: They have forsaken Me, the fountain of living waters, And hewn themselves cisterns—broken cisterns that can hold no water* (Jeremiah 2:13).

Immediately after I read this verse, the Lord took me into a vision. I saw a fountain with water flowing out of it. There were lots of people around the fountain drinking, splashing, and having a good time. I noticed that the flow of the water was strong at times and ebbed at other times. At its strongest flow, it actually sprayed over the edges of the bowl; and when it ebbed, there was barely a trickle running down the fountain, but it still supplied the bowl. The people noticed this change in flow too. Someone said, "Let's go build a cistern to hold the water. You never know, the fountain may stop someday and then we would be out of water. Plus, it's being wasted when it flows over the bowl."

So the people went some distance from the fountain and built a cistern. They got buckets and started taking the water from the fountain to the cistern. When the cistern was filled, they went about with their lives and took their water from the cistern instead of the fountain.

However, there was a problem. This cistern had a leak. It was a slow leak, so the people didn't realize that the water level was dropping. When new people came around who hadn't seen the full cistern, they just thought it was at the level it had always been. Over a long period of time, the water was reduced to mere puddles in the bottom of the cistern. People had to lie on the ground and reach down into the cistern in order to get some water. By this time the water had grown stagnant, but the people didn't even notice that the water tasted foul because they had become dulled to what the water was like in the beginning.

Then someone finally remembered the fountain and got every-one excited. They traveled back to the fountain, which wasn't far. The water was still flowing, and they raced to it, drinking, splashing, and having a good time. They were revived. But eventually the cycle started all over again. Someone said, "Let's go build a cistern to hold the water...."

This gives us a picture of revival history. The water represents the move of the Holy Spirit. There are those who say the same things about the move of God that people said about the fountain. When the water overflowed onto the ground, people said that it was being wasted. They assumed it was unnecessary or perhaps dangerous. No doubt it was muddy around the fountain. Messy. Perhaps the excessive water caused weeds to grow around the fountain. God caused the fountain to flow at the pressure He desired.

Why did the people build a cistern? Fear! "What if the water stops?" they asked. Fear brings distrust of the Trustworthy One. Notice what God said through Jeremiah: *They have forsaken Me, the fountain of living waters...."*

God is the fountain, and the fountain is ours forever. Is it possible for God to ever dry up? Psalm 37:3 says, *"Trust in the Lord, and do good; dwell in the land, and feed on His faithfulness."* Don't forsake Him because you don't understand everything or because you think something negative may happen in the future. Have faith that God truly does know best! When the water is flowing very slowly and it looks like it may stop, it is time for our faith to step up to the plate. God said He would never leave us. His fountain will never stop and it will never dry up. The bowl will never be empty. The slow seasons are opportunities for us to learn to appreciate the overflowing times more. Certainly He wants us to learn to trust Him whether things are flowing fast or slow.

The cistern is a picture of how we try to control and contain what God is doing. When we open the door to fear, we allow a spirit of control to enter. Whatever you control becomes stagnant. It may happen over a long or short period of time, but it will happen every time. When we don't trust God, we do things our way. We try to control what He's given us. The problem with trying to control things is that it extinguishes the move of the Holy Spirit. This grieves Him because it communicates that we do not trust Him and merely want the benefits of His presence instead of His presence itself. How could we desire anything more than His presence?

Note that Jeremiah says forsaking the fountain and building cisterns are two evils. These aren't just little mistakes or sins; they are actually described as "evils." One of the meanings of *evil* in Hebrew is "destroy." Fear and control destroy the works of God.

POINTS TO PONDER

1. What is the most significant difference between a fountain and a cistern? How does this portray spiritual vitality? Have you ever kept water in a cistern, a trough, or even a birdbath? What happened to it before long?

    ....

    ....

    ....

    ....

2. In light of what Jeremiah wrote, what does Psalm 68:26 mean? It reads: *"Bless God in the congregations, the Lord, from the fountain of Israel."*

    ....

    ....

    ....

    ....

3. Do you know what it means to desire God's presence itself more than the benefits of His presence? Do you also know what it means to desire the benefits of His presence more than God Himself?

    ....

    ....

    ....

    ....

MEDITATION

If the fountain is overflowing, perhaps the water soaking into the ground is forming a reservoir that will provide a well for someone in the future. Maybe Someone will come along and use the mud to give sight to a blind man. Perhaps what we assume to be weeds are really beautiful flowering plants instead.

Ask God to keep your heart as soft as the soil around an overflowing fountain of His presence. Ask Him to let His fountain flow however He wants it to flow in your life and the life of the congregation you are a part of.

Chapter 35

START YOUR OWN HERITAGE

Eric Johnson

Tʜᴇ Oʟᴅ Tᴇsᴛᴀᴍᴇɴᴛ ᴇᴍᴘʜᴀsɪᴢᴇs inheritance coming from the bloodline of a family. In the New Testament, we see a shift: we are grafted into the family of God when we believe in Him, no matter what our bloodline is.

Paul explains it simply: we have been adopted as sons and daughters and have been blessed with every spiritual blessing according to the riches of His grace (see Eph. 1:3-8). So even if we don't have great bloodlines that are rich with inheritance, we get grafted into the greatest inheritance in the universe.

Often when I teach on this topic, someone will approach me and say, "I don't have an inheritance, and my family is not one to be proud of."

My usual response is, "That's perfect!" Of course, they are usually taken aback. The reason it's perfect is because those without a natural inheritance have been presented with one of the greatest opportunities of life—to start their own heritage. We serve a redeeming God; He is the God of the redeemed. Our ability to start a heritage and a legacy is all rooted in the fact that our Daddy loves redemption.

Jeremiah 12:15 reads:

> *Then it shall be, after I have plucked them out, that I will return and have compassion on them and bring them back, everyone to his heritage and everyone to his land.*

God promises to return us to our inheritance, even after uprooting us from bad soil. We serve a redeeming God who is in the business of placing us back into our inheritance. We have been grafted into God's family.

This past year I had the opportunity of interviewing my dad's mom in front of our first- and second-year class at Bethel School of Supernatural Ministry. The purpose of this time was for her to share some of the history and heritage that have helped create the environment that the students are now living in. During this time, she handed out to every student a piece of paper that had a list of family Scriptures. These passages of Scripture were Bible promises that we have embraced and declared over our families through the years.

When my grandma handed this paper out, she said, "These are now your promises for you and your families." What took place was that she gave the class an inheritance that became theirs. Her ceiling became their floor.

Here are some of the scriptural promises that my family members for generations have held onto and released over our homes and lives. Take these verses and declare them over yourself and your families. Let this become the foundation you build on:

> *But as for me and my house, we will serve the Lord* (Joshua 24:15).

> *The counsel of the Lord stands forever, the plans of His heart to all generations* (Psalm 33:11).

> *Let Your work appear to Your servants, and Your glory to their children* (Psalm 90:16).

The Lord is good; His mercy is everlasting, and His truth endures to all generations (Psalm 100:5).

Children are a heritage from the Lord, the fruit of the womb is a reward (Psalm 127:3).

In the fear of the Lord there is strong confidence, and His children will have a place of refuge (Proverbs 14:26).

His mercy is on those who fear Him from generation to generation (Luke 1:50).

And it shall come to pass in the last days, says God, that I will pour out of My Spirit on all flesh; your sons and your daughters shall prophesy, your young men shall see visions, your old men shall dream dreams (Acts 2:17).

Believe on the Lord Jesus Christ, and you will be saved, you and your household (Acts 16:31).

To intentionally live for generations we will never see is both an incredible opportunity and a huge responsibility. When people begin to walk in a fresh understanding of an abundant God, they begin naturally to live for generations that will follow them. But when people reduce the Christian life to just their own lives, or they are consumed with lack, they often lose the very ability to do this.

History teaches us something: What cost one generation dearly will often cost the next generation nothing. As we begin a heritage, we have to be willing to accept the fact that we may spend our entire lives building something, and then it will be the next generation's decision to advance with what we laid down for them.

POINTS TO PONDER

1. How are natural inheritance and spiritual inheritance different? How do they overlap? What has been your experience with both kinds of inheritance?

    ....

    ....

    ....

    ....

2. Where do you find yourself in the heritage-building business? Did you receive a godly inheritance from your parents and previous generations, or have you had to start from scratch? Where you find yourself will influence your own heritage-building.

    ....

    ....

    ....

    ....

3. Which of the scriptural promises above can you claim with the most enthusiasm? What makes it special to you?

    ....

    ....

    ....

    ....

MEDITATION

When people talk about a material inheritance, they often note, "You can't take it with you," which is true. Yet they often neglect the most important kind of inheritance—salvation and redemption—which you *can* take with you. This spiritual inheritance is not just pie in the sky in the by-and-by. It begins instantly and supplies all that you need to live a Kingdom life. When "invested" fruitfully, your inheritance from God—whether you are building on what has come to you from previous generations or starting fresh—will yield abundant returns so that you can in turn pass on a good inheritance to your physical and/or spiritual children.

As you claim for your own family the scriptural promises listed above and make them your own, you might want to look up some of them in various translations of the Bible. Sometimes the substitution of a single word can reveal new depths of meaning and can make a promise become more personal.

Chapter 36

PRAYER THAT WORKS

Kevin Dedmon

IN A SENSE, ALL religions of the world attempt to influence their god(s) to intervene on their behalf. I spent two weeks ministering in India, where hundreds of gods are worshiped for protection, provision, healing, and every other need known to people. On one occasion, we went to a place where about 30 million men make a pilgrimage each year during a two-week window, crawling on their stomachs, cutting themselves, and chanting prescribed mantras in hopes of influencing six rocks stationed on top of a hill to bless them with their supposed supernatural powers.

Year after year, they make the same journey to worship these rocks with the same unanswered results, yet they continue in their futile petitions, hoping for a breakthrough. It is like the definition of insanity that's attributed to Albert Einstein: "Doing the same [failing] thing over and over again and expecting different results."

It is in this context that Jesus advised us not to keep on babbling like pagans, who think they will be heard because of their many words. (See Matthew 6:7.) Effectiveness of prayer for the pagans, then, is to pray the right words for a long time. But prayers based on length and repetition are not the key to releasing God's Kingdom.

Jesus also warned His disciples not to pray like the hypocrites, referring most likely to the religious leaders of the day, who would pray for show. (See Matthew 6:5.) Eloquence and outward displays of devotion are equally ineffective in influencing God to intervene for our needs and desires. Religious prayers are not the answer to changing the world.

In the days of Jesus, the Jewish religious leaders had come up with several prayers that they were sure would influence God to bless them. These prayers had to be memorized and spoken with perfect accuracy in order to be effective. They were the formula to move Heaven to earth.

For example, the Shema (found in Deuteronomy 6:4-9), had to be quoted out loud two times a day to ensure God's blessing. The Amidah, also known as the Eighteen Blessings, was to be quoted word-for-word once a day. When printed out on 8½ x 11-inch paper, the Amidah covers seven pages!

Then there were the various forms of the Kaddish, which were written prayers that, when recited properly, were to release specific blessings for every occasion and need in life. There was the Sabbath Kaddish, the Passover Kaddish, a Wedding Kaddish, and a Funeral Kaddish, just to mention a few. The Jewish repertoire of religious prayers covered every base to ensure that God would move Heaven to earth for them.

Jesus simplified prayer for His disciples. He taught them how to move Heaven to meet our daily needs, *"Give us this day our daily bread"* (Matt. 6:11), whether for nutritional sustenance, emotional fortitude or comfort, spiritual renewal, miraculous intervention in circumstances, or physical healing. He instructed them to influence Heaven to bring relational reconciliation by praying, *"Forgive us our debts, as we forgive our debtors"* (Matt. 6:12). He taught them to bring Heaven to earth in order to overcome the powers of the evil one by praying, *"Deliver us from the evil one..."* (Matt. 6:13).

The point that Jesus was making to His disciples in Matthew 6 was that the kind of prayer that influences God does not involve whipping up the right words, the proper formula, or the perfect technique. Living a naturally supernatural life, releasing God's Kingdom, moving Heaven to earth, is a result of living in dynamic, intimate relationship with God.

When Jesus instructed His disciples to pray, *"Our Father in heaven, hallowed be Your name. Your kingdom come. Your will be done on earth as it is in heaven"* (Matt. 6:9-10), He was teaching them how to influence Heaven to come to earth. He was teaching them how to petition God to release His Kingdom, bringing intervention in the affairs of people.

The goal of this kind of petition prayer is to change something, to move something, to influence God to intervene where people cannot. It is asking God for miracle breakthrough where there is no hope. It is causing Heaven to invade earth so that His Kingdom comes, so that His will is done on earth as it is in Heaven. The words themselves may vary, but the heart of the person praying echoes the intentions of God's own heart.

This is our prayer model, and moving Heaven to earth is our goal.

POINTS TO PONDER

1. Why do you think that people have a tendency to invent and re-ly on repeating rote prayers and religious actions? Have you no-ticed this tendency in yourself or in those around you?

    ....

    ....

    ....

    ....

2. How is the Lord's Prayer (which you can find in Matthew 6:9-13 and Luke 11:2-4) different from any other often-repeated prayer for which the words have been prescribed ahead of time? How can some other traditional prayer move into the realm of true prayer and communication with God? What makes the difference?

    ....

    ....

    ....

    ....

3. What does it mean to "move Heaven to earth"? How do our prayers accomplish this?

    ....

    ....

    ....

    ....

MEDITATION

Meditate on each line as you pray the Lord's Prayer as found in Matthew 6:9-13. Look for immediate, personal applications for the various aspects of the prayer:

> *Our Father in heaven, hallowed be Your name. Your kingdom come. Your will be done on earth as it is in heaven. Give us this day our daily bread. And forgive us our debts, as we forgive our debtors. And do not lead us into temptation, but deliver us from the evil one. For Yours is the kingdom and the power and the glory forever. Amen.*

Chapter 37

MANTLE—OR MORE?

Bill Johnson

Personally, I get nauseated over those who claim to have the mantle of Smith Wigglesworth or any other hero of the faith. First of all, if it were true, let someone else say it. It should never be our claim to make. Second, the goal is not for us to be identified by the nature of another person's gift. It is to draw and build upon previous breakthroughs so that we can step into the full purpose of God for us and for our generation. God doesn't want or need another Wigglesworth, as great as he was. He wants you and me, as we are, surrendered to His purposes, utilizing the breakthroughs of the generations that have gone before us to accomplish something new.

What He has planned for us is much bigger than we think—and impossible to achieve through determination alone. In fact, it will take the sanctified efforts of multiple generations to accomplish our God-given assignment. It's even bigger than the need for unity among the generations that are privileged to be alive at the same time. It will take a rediscovery of the concept of spiritual inheritance through the unity of generations past and present. This is done only through true unity of the Spirit, for He alone knows the intended heartbeat of each generation.

There were kings who followed after David who received special treatment from God simply because they were his descendants. David had obtained such a place of victory and favor before God that it became a corporate blessing, both to those under his rule and those in the generations to follow. Tragically, most of the succeeding kings didn't value the inheritance they received and got caught up in the power and privilege of their position.

An inheritance gives people an advantage, if they will use it correctly. But it will cost them dearly if they don't. These descendants of David started life with position and great favor with God. Favor with God is the greatest inheritance, apart from the actual presence of God. It is money in the bank in the Kingdom economy. But as it is in the natural, so it is in the spiritual. Having money in the bank doesn't mean I will use it correctly. And many have suffered shipwreck due to mismanagement of their spiritual inheritance.

Preachers' kids are notorious for sinful and rebellious behavior. Is it possible that they are a primary target for the powers of darkness because of the favor they carry and their position to be in line for an inheritance to build upon? Their access to spiritual inheritance is a great threat to the dark realm. And so, like the privileged few who inherit millions and live without restraint, this special breed of people gets sidetracked from their purpose.

Sometimes they miss their call because of a double standard that is lived in the preacher's home. It ends up undermining the destiny of the children. If they see one message preached from the pulpit and quite another lived at home, they use the discrepancy as the justification to abandon the life of faith preached by the parents. And then again, it is sometimes caused by church members who play right into the devil's hands through their criticisms and unsanctified requirements placed on the children of men and women of God. The stories of such failures are, regrettably, many.

Religion is form without power. It is cruel and boring and has taken the lives of many young people who had great potential in God.

Inheritance reveals purpose. We are blessed to live at a time when the tide is turning and more and more people are learning how to capitalize on their place in life. More and more descendants of the mighty are in fact rising to their potential.

What once caused a person to stand out as an unusually gifted person should become the new standard for the Body of Christ through the process of equipping the saints. This is spiritual inheritance made practical. It happens directly through training, discipleship, and impartation, and indirectly through honor, respect, study, and prayer.

That is what Moses meant when he said, *"Oh, that all the Lord's people were prophets and that the Lord would put His Spirit upon them"* (Num. 11:29). Besides adjusting Joshua's thinking, Moses was prophesying of a future day when the Spirit would be released upon all God's people, creating a new standard for what could be accomplished by the average believer.

This means that the extraordinary anointing upon one would become the possession and experience of all. This has incomprehensible possibilities.

POINTS TO PONDER

1. Who holds your inheritance in trust for you? Have you reached the "age of maturity" yet? Are you ready and willing to assume more responsibility than before? Can you lay aside your insufficient notions about what it means to inherit a call and an anointing?

    ....

    ....

    ....

    ....

2. Is it wrong to talk in terms of impartations or mantles? Where do such things fit into the bigger picture?

    ....

    ....

    ....

    ....

3. Were the highly esteemed saints who have gone before you perfect in every way? What made them different from other imperfect human beings? What is the best way for you to follow in their footsteps?

    ....

    ....

    ....

    ....

MEDITATION

The possibilities within God's Kingdom are ever-expanding and always bigger than anything we can imagine. Why limit yourself to an "impartation" or a "mantle" when you have an unlimited supply of God's power available to be perfectly expressed through you?

Granted, no one person can contain or express it all. That's why you have brothers and sisters in Christ, past and present, across the globe. But in unity with them, you can do your part to live within your heavenly Father's inheritance—and serve as a trustee for the sake of others.

Repent for your narrow interpretation of what it means to walk in your full inheritance. Gratefully allow your Father the pleasure of escorting you to a new level of sonship.

Chapter 38

ALL IN A DAY'S WORK

Banning Liebscher

FROM VERY EARLY ON at our Jesus Culture conferences, we realized that it would be ineffective to teach people that they belong to a new breed of revivalists without actually giving them a chance to experience it. People need to be motivated and encouraged to just get out there, receive a word of knowledge, and pray for people to have an encounter with God.

Perhaps my favorite testimony of all happened at one of our Redding conferences. Before this group of young people left the church, their leader had them wait on the Holy Spirit to download words of knowledge. On this occasion, a teenage girl said she saw in her mind's eye a picture of a broken tree.

Their group was dropped off in a grocery store parking lot, but they couldn't see anything similar to the girl's description. They decided to walk into a neighborhood to attempt to find the tree. As they strolled through the streets, they saw a plumber standing by his van. The group approached him and asked if he needed prayer for anything. Immediately, he blurted out, "Yes, my wife is an alcoholic." (This shows how desperate people can be, so much so that in this case, a grown man would confide in a group of teenagers about his situation at home.) They bowed their heads with him and prayed for his wife.

During the prayer, one of them received a word of knowledge about knee pain, so after they finished praying, that one inquired if he had anything wrong with his knees. He looked at them in astonishment and asked, "How did you know I have knee problems?"

They responded, "Sir, God speaks to us, and He told us you have knee problems." They asked if they could pray for that, and he said yes, so they knelt down, laid their hands on his knees, and prayed for the power of God to be released. One of them prayed, "God, heal his knees. Take the water off the knees and restore the cartilage."

The man stepped back, shocked. "How did you know I have water on my knees and how did you know I have missing cartilage?"

They said, "Sir, we already told you: God speaks to us." They asked if he would test it out. The plumber moved up and down and realized that all the pain had left his knees. He had been healed.

The teenagers blessed him and then moved on to find the broken tree. On the way, they ran into a highly unusual circumstance in which they felt led to phone a telephone number on a handmade flyer that had been posted in a public place. In that case, their leader prayed with the man who answered the phone for deliverance, and helped him understand what was happening.

As the team moved down the street after the phone call, the girl recognized the tree. She shouted out, "Look, there it is! Behind that gas station. That's the tree I saw." They felt that God had something for them in the gas station convenience store. The group walked in and one of them asked, "Does anyone in here have a pain in their neck?"

Two ladies were working behind the counter. One of them sarcastically responded with, "The only pain in the neck around here is my boss," and walked off.

They approached the other woman and said, "Well, that is not exactly what we meant. Do you have a pain in your neck?" She hesitantly admitted that she did. The group knew the Lord had brought them there to minister to her, so they asked, "Would you mind if we prayed for you?"

She pointed at a security camera in the corner and said, "I don't think my boss would like that. I would get in trouble."

Refusing to be turned down, the leader of the group suggested, "Well, what if we act like we are buying a pack of gum? Slide your hand over to us and we will pray for you."

She agreed. While they were praying, one of the teens heard another word of knowledge regarding her family. "You have been experiencing relational strife in your family. You've been carrying this weight for your family recently, so much so that it is manifesting in a physical pain in your shoulders." The lady began to weep. They ministered the love of Jesus to her and encouraged her in what God had for her family.

That was just a normal day in the lives of this new breed of risk-taking revivalists. Everywhere they go, they are looking for chances to bring people into an encounter with God. As you can see, though, most of the time these opportunities lie on the other side of a risk, and you need to be creative sometimes as you persist in your efforts to follow what the Spirit is telling you.

POINTS TO PONDER

1. Do stories like these make you want to "go and do likewise"? What might be holding you back?

   ....

   ....

   ....

   ....

2. Have you ever approached a stranger to offer to pray for him or her? Has anyone ever approached you with such an offer? How do such experiences—or the lack of such experiences—fit together with what you feel God is calling you to do in your daily life?

   ....

   ....

   ....

   ....

3. Think about the demeanor of the team members in these stories. How would you characterize their overall behavior? What can you learn from this?

   ....

   ....

   ....

   ....

MEDITATION

We were born to live in the realm of the supernatural—the realm of healings, prophetic utterances, angelic encounters, and the gifts of the Spirit. It should be the most *natural* thing for a Christian to live a *super-natural* lifestyle. If you feel dissatisfied with your Christian walk, it may be because you are missing this all-important element.

Jesus didn't only invite Peter to walk on the water (see Matt. 14:22-33). By inviting him to risk walking on water, Jesus was inviting Peter into the realm He lived in all the time—the realm of the supernatural. And He welcomes us to live there as well. Jesus is looking at you just as He looked at Peter and He is saying, "Come." He is inviting you to live a supernatural life. Can you hear Him calling?

Chapter 39

WAITING FOR THE BRIDEGROOM

Paul Manwaring

THINK OF IT—FOR ALL eternity we will be the daughter-in-law of God! That describes one aspect of how we become joint heirs with Jesus. We fall in love, take the family name, and like daughters-in-law, become joint heirs with the Son.

More than any other New Testament writer, the apostle John used bridal imagery in describing our relationship with Christ, particularly in his Gospel and in the Book of Revelation. It begins when he quotes John the Baptist: *"He who has the bride is the bridegroom; but the friend of the bridegroom, who stands and hears him, rejoices greatly because of the bridegroom's voice..."* (John 3:29). The New International Version says the friend *"waits and listens for"* the bridegroom.

Why does the "friend of the bridegroom" wait for the bridegroom's voice? At that time in Jewish culture, the tradition was that the engagement was the most important event—the decision you couldn't retract from. You couldn't decide to take the ring back to Zales and get your money back, because once you were engaged, you were engaged. That was it. Following that event, the bridegroom went back to his father's house to prepare the place for them to live. The bridegroom left his good friend, the best man, with the bride to make sure that she was kept pure and to help her get ready for marriage. That is why he was the best man! He was the one whom the groom could trust with his most valuable relationship, his bride-to-be. And when he heard the bridegroom's voice again, he knew it was time to deliver the bride to him.

The picture is beautiful and helps us to understand the language of the Gospels. Jesus said:

> In My Father's house are many mansions [literally, "dwellings"]; if it were not so, I would have told you. I go to prepare a place for you. And if I go and prepare a place for you, I will come again and receive you to Myself; that where I am, there you may be also (John 14:2-3).

In His death and resurrection, Christ made a covenant with the Bride—that's us—betrothing us to Himself for eternity, and then He left the Spirit of truth with us to keep us pure and get us ready for His return. The Holy Spirit is waiting with us in great anticipation for the Groom's voice; this is why *"the Spirit and the bride say, 'Come!'"* (Rev. 22:17a).

History culminates with a wedding, and we should celebrate this when we go to weddings and see all the ways they remind us of the great joy that awaits us. But that great wedding is only the beginning of an eternal marriage. For this reason, marriage is the pinnacle reflection of eternal relationships. Marriage is a glory-carrier, revealing the passionate commitment of Heaven to an agenda of endless love. Marriage is our tutor on the way to the marriage supper of the Lamb.

The culture of divorce that has developed over the last half-century has been devastating to all of us, and restoring people who divorce is a vital ministry of the Church. But even as we see the ways people fall short of entering into God's design for marriage, we must not let go of the fact that lifelong marriage is the goal! I submit that we would do much in addressing the problem of bad marriages and divorce by spending more time looking at the love of Christ and then at how right and beautiful marriage is when it expresses that love. There are couples among us who have celebrated as many as 60 or 70 years of covenant love together, love that has only grown stronger as it has weathered the ups and downs of life. Their lives are the greatest canvas displaying what the love of Jesus, our Groom, looks like—love that endures despite our betrayals and rebellions and love of other gods—love that is willing to shed its own blood. We must endeavor to keep this picture of marriage before us, for what we behold, we become!

In our independent culture, we often forget and, therefore, miss the advantages of the fact that marriage is also an adoption. The groom is adopted by his bride's parents and she by his. As a result of this connection, the children that result from their marriage are connected through their parents, not just to a chain of relationships, but to an entire tapestry of relationships through which, when they express the design of God, bring multiplied life and blessing to each generation.

POINTS TO PONDER

1. Do you appreciate the idea of being the daughter-in-law of Father God for all of eternity? What do you like about that idea? What, if anything, seems less attractive about it? Evaluate your reactions and see what God says to you.

    ....

    ....

    ....

    ....

2. When the love of husbands truly reflects Christ's love for the Church as Paul instructed (see Eph. 5:25), then wives experience the joy in submitting to their husbands that we experience in submitting our lives to Christ and entering into the safety and freedom of following His lead in life. Reflect on the fact that marriage is the interplay of love and submission, as is our divine union with Christ Jesus.

    ....

    ....

    ....

    ....

3. How is every marriage also an adoption, especially in the Kingdom?

    ....

    ....

    ....

    ....

MEDITATION

We can only give what we have received. We cannot expect to love one another like Christ until we have learned to be loved by Him, to experience the reality of how He loves us. This is why the apostle Paul not only told us what our love is to look like, but also, in the same letter, prayed a powerful apostolic prayer for us:

> *For this reason I bow my knees to the Father of our Lord Jesus Christ, from whom the whole family in heaven and earth is named, that He would grant you, according to the riches of His glory, to be strengthened with might through His Spirit in the inner man, that Christ may dwell in your hearts through faith; that you, being rooted and grounded in love, may be able to comprehend with all the saints what is the width and length and depth and height—to know the love of Christ which passes knowledge; that you may be filled with all the fullness of God* (Ephesians 3:14-19).

Receive the answer to this prayer in your own life. Seek to know the love of Christ and depend hard on His power in your inner person to bring you into the fullness of that love. The marriage feast awaits you!

Chapter 40

WATCH OVER YOUR HEART

Bill Johnson

DAILY, WE LIVE IN the crossroads—that place between mystery and revelation. My job is to trust my heavenly father with the problems and situations I don't understand and to focus on stewarding my will to what I know to be true. My success in watching over my heart determines the measure of Kingdom breakthrough I will experience in my life. In other words, my internal reality often defines the nature of my external reality; if I prosper in my heart, my life will prosper.

Strengthening ourselves in the Lord is an essential part of stewarding our hearts. The tools that I have learned to use to strengthen myself in the Lord have become calculated responses to the warning lights of my heart. But the fact is, I can only respond correctly if I already recognize and understand the signals my heart sends. If the oil light comes on in my car, and my response is to take it to the car wash, I clearly do not understand what the light means. Worse yet, the real problem has not been dealt with and will soon manifest in a breakdown.

When it comes to my heart, I have found that the only way I can correctly use the tools I've received to strengthen myself is to establish foundational truths in my thinking—truths about the nature of reality, who God is, and who He has made me to be. These truths help me identify my heart signals.

How do you know that your thinking and your heart are intimately connected? The Western mindset compartmentalizes human beings when it comes to feelings and thinking—the heart feels and the mind thinks. But Scripture says, *"For as he thinks in his heart, so is he..."* (Prov. 23:7). In fact, the Hebrew definition of the word *heart* encompasses the entirety of your "inner self." Your heart is the seat of your mind, imagination, will, desires, emotions, affections, memories, and conscience. It is also the center of your communion with the Spirit of God, and it possesses the faculties that perceive spiritual reality. The New International Version refers to this spiritual perception as "the eyes of your heart" (see Eph. 1:18) Thus, your heart is what enables you to have faith, which is the *"evidence of things not seen"* (Heb. 11:1). Your faith grows as your heart, led by the Holy Spirit, perceives and understands the invisible realms of spiritual reality. That unseen realm governs the visible realm and brings your mind and will into agreement with the reality of the Kingdom. In essence, what I have just described is the process of renewing the mind.

What gives permission for that reality to flow into the issues of our lives? Our internal focus on and agreement with spiritual reality—either the reality of God's Kingdom, established on the truth, or the destructive reality of the enemy's kingdom, established on lies.

This power of agreement with spiritual reality through our focus adds another dimension to the principle that life flows from the heart: *you become what you behold.* God has made clear what we are becoming— the potential we are all called to grow into throughout our lifetimes. We are becoming kings and priests of the planet, following the lead of our Elder Brother, Jesus. This is why Hebrews tells us to fix our eyes on Jesus (see Heb. 12:2). Our goal is to sustain our focus on Him because we become like the One we behold. The degree to which we understand our identity and purpose—who we are becoming—is always determined by the degree of our revelation of Jesus. He is the exact representation of the Father, in whose image we were created.

Beholding Jesus cannot be reduced to reading about Him in the Scriptures. He died so that the same Spirit who was in and upon Him, giving Him constant access to what the Father was saying and doing, could be sent to live in us. The truth is that every believer has constant access to the manifest presence of God. We are an open Heaven.

But we have to take advantage of that access, and we do that by turning our focus on Him. Only in that place of communion with Him do we come to *know* Him and, consequently, to gain the revelation of our identity and purpose. And as we agree with the revelation of who He is, the reality of who He is starts to flow into our lives and transform us into His likeness. All fruitfulness in our lives flows from this place of intimacy with the Lord.

POINTS TO PONDER

1. In terms of your ability to read the signals of your heart, how have you changed as you have matured in the Lord? In your own words, see if you can describe how your heart has facilitated the renewing of your mind.

    ....

    ....

    ....

    ....

2. In your own life, how do you see the truth of the statement, "you become what you behold"?

    ....

    ....

    ....

    ....

3. Keeping in mind what you have just read, ponder the meaning of Jesus' words when He said, *"You shall love the Lord your God with all your heart, with all your soul, and with all your mind"* (Matt. 22:37).

    ....

    ....

    ....

    ....

MEDITATION

Keeping tabs on all the different aspects of the Christian life can be overwhelming. There is a seemingly endless list of responsibilities to attend to. There is the issue of relationships inside and outside of your immediate family, your place of employment, ministry, community involvement, and evangelism. And then there's the issue of Christian disciplines such as prayer, personal Bible study, witnessing, corporate gatherings, fasting—the list goes on and on. To make matters worse, most of us are quite capable of making simple things very complex. Yet Jesus illustrated a simple lifestyle, one that is carefree and yet not irresponsible—simple without cares.

Solomon seemed to recognize a key to this great Kingdom lifestyle when he said, *"Keep your heart with all diligence, for out of it spring the issues of life"* (Prov. 4:23). All the issues of your life flow like rivers from one central location—your heart—and what you do to steward that one place determines the outcome of your life.

Respond once again to God's invitation to offer Him your very heart. Respond to His living presence as He remodels your spirit into a better dwelling place for His Spirit.

About the Authors

Bill Johnson is a fifth-generation pastor with a rich heritage in the Holy Spirit. Bill and his wife, Beni are the senior pastors of Bethel Church in Redding, California. They serve a growing number of churches that have partnered for revival through a leadership network that crosses denominational lines and builds relationships. Beni oversees Bethel's intercessors and Prayer House. Her approach to intercession makes supernatural connections with the Lord accessible to all. Bill and Beni's three children and their spouses are all involved in full-time ministry. They have eight wonderful grandchildren.

Eric Johnson serves on the senior leadership team for Bethel Church and is also the senior overseer for the second-year Bethel Supernatural School of Ministry. Eric is a sixth-generation pastor with a hunger to see people experience the power of God in their lives. His wife, Candace and he have a passion to see the transformation of nations. One of their chief joys in life is raising their two beautiful daughters, Kennedy and Selah.

Danny Silk serves as a senior management pastor at Bethel Church. He is a primary developer of the staff team and director of the church ministries, including the Transformation Center, city outreach, and Bethel's Healing Rooms. Danny and his wife, Sheri are also the founders of Loving On Purpose, a ministry to families and communities around the world.

Kevin Dedmon has a traveling ministry focused on equipping, empowering, and activating the Church for supernatural evangelism through signs and wonders, healing, and the prophetic. He earned a Master's degree in church leadership from Vanguard University, and has been in full-time ministry for more than 25 years. He and his wife are part of the Bethel Church staff.

Chris Overstreet serves as the outreach pastor of Bethel Church and its School of Supernatural Ministry. It is common for miracles, salvations and life transformations to occur as Chris lives his life in the realm of the naturally supernatural. Chris and his wife, Stefanie, a registered nurse, have a heart for missions. They travel globally, equipping ordinary people in supernatural evangelism.

Banning and *SeaJay Liebscher* have been on staff at Bethel Church for over ten years. They are the directors of Jesus Culture, a ministry dedicated to mobilizing, equipping, activating, and sending a new breed of revivalist all over the world. These revivalists are encountering God, burning with passion for Jesus, being trained and equipped in the realm of the supernatural, and being sent into their cities to minister in power. Prior to his current position, Banning was the youth pastor at Bethel Church and a lead overseer in the School of Supernatural Ministry.

Judy Franklin works for Pastor Bill Johnson of Bethel Church. Her experiences with God have made her a bridge for many into the invisible realm. She has a heart for showing others how to have an intimate relationship with God. She has three children, seven grandchildren and one great-grandchild.

Chad Dedmon has had full-time pastoral experience working with youth and young adults. Chad and his wife, Julia were ordained as ministers of the Gospel of Jesus Christ by Drs. Rolland and Heidi Baker of Iris Ministries and senior leaders Bill and Beni Johnson of Bethel Church. They reside in Orange County, California, and travel worldwide as ministers.

Paul Manwaring is on the senior leadership team at Bethel Church and oversees Global Legacy, Bethel's apostolic relational network. He passionately pursues glory on earth, lives and organizations being transformed, and the secular/sacred dividing line erased. Paul spent 19 years in senior prison management in England, is a registered general and psychiatric nurse, and holds a Master of Studies in management from Cambridge University.